THE dinghy BIBLE

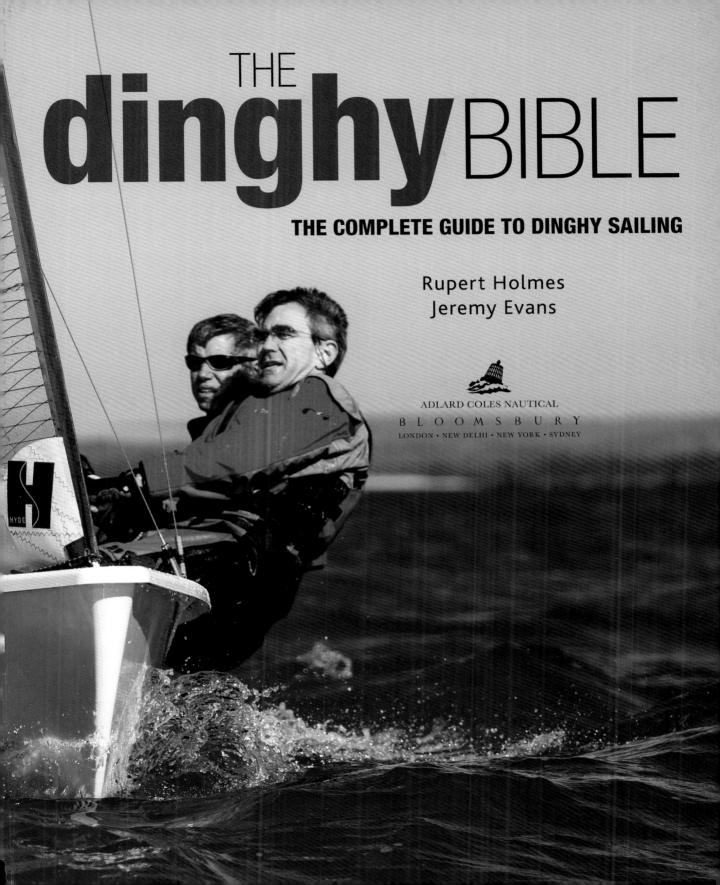

THE
dinghy BIBLE

THE COMPLETE GUIDE TO DINGHY SAILING

Rupert Holmes
Jeremy Evans

ADLARD COLES NAUTICAL
BLOOMSBURY
LONDON · NEW DELHI · NEW YORK · SYDNEY

Published by Adlard Coles Nautical
an imprint of Bloomsbury Publishing Plc
50 Bedford Square, London WC1B 3DP
www.adlardcoles.com

Copyright © Adlard Coles Nautical 2014
First edition 2014

ISBN 978-1-4081-8800-2

A CIP catalogue record for this book is available from the
British Library.

This book is produced using paper that is made from
wood grown in managed, sustainable forests. It is natural,
renewable and recyclable. The logging and manufacturing
processes conform to the environmental regulations of the
country of origin.

Produced for Adlard Coles Nautical by Ivy Contract.

Art director: Kevin Knight
Senior editor: Judith Chamberlain-Webber
Designer: Nicola Liddiard

Typeset in Bliss and Antenna
Printed in China by C & C Offset Printing Co.

Contents

Welcome to dinghy sailing   8

Welcome to dinghy sailing

There are a huge number of different facets to dinghy sailing, encompassing everything from gentle after-work pottering on a quiet summer's evening to competitive racing right up to Olympic level.

There are as many different motivations for dinghy sailing as there are sailors. While some are unquestionably thrill seekers who revel in pitting their skills against the elements on the windiest of days, others are quiet nature lovers wanting to get closer to the environment. Those with a competitive streak are focussed on winning major championships, or even an Olympic gold medal.

While some hardened enthusiasts from all disciplines of sailing invest huge amounts of time and money on their activities afloat, this is by no means universal and for most participants dinghy sailing is a perfectly manageable activity, both in terms of time and money.

It's also a family-friendly pursuit that's suitable for people of all ages – with a little training, children as young as seven or eight can successfully sail alone in a small, singlehanded boat, or crew a larger dinghy. Equally, there are many dinghy sailors who are a decade or more past retirement age, in some of the fastest and most technologically advanced designs.

It's perhaps therefore no surprise that there are many families in which everyone is hooked on dinghy sailing – it's an experience which all members can share.

Below: **High-level racing is the inspiration for some dinghy sailors.**

First steps

Most people get their first experience of dinghy sailing through one of three routes: an introduction from a friend who already sails, a course at a local sailing club or watersports centre, or a holiday in the sun.

All are routes that will enable you to get a taste for sailing without needing to invest in your own boat or expensive gear. Indeed, even when you become more experienced it's not essential to own a boat – every owner of a two-handed dinghy or catamaran needs a crew to help sail it, so competent people are always in demand.

Buying a boat

When it comes to the time that you want to own your first boat, it's possible to buy a second-hand dinghy for a three-figure sum, and even well looked after newer models frequently change hands for no more than the price of an ageing second-hand car.

Above: **Even quite young children can master basic sailing with a little help.**

As for other costs, many dinghy sailors use the facilities of a club – membership rarely costs more than a few hundred pounds a year for a couple or family, including a place to keep a boat in the dinghy park. Don't worry about being accepted for membership of a club – only the most exclusive have waiting lists and most are very welcoming to new members, and run a number of training courses and open days.

Left: **Some dinghy sailors enjoy cruising, or just pottering around for a few hours on a low-tech boat.**

First steps

Where to sail safely

Launching off a sandy beach onto smooth water with a fair wind and warm sun sounds like sailing perfection. But everything is not always as it appears. The sand may be too soft to push your boat to the water, the water may shelve steeply from the shoreline, rocks may be hidden beneath the surface, or perhaps there's no one to help if things go wrong.

Sailing clubs

Join a sailing club and enjoy the following benefits:

- ✪ The club will be situated in a good sailing location. If you have problems with rigging, launching, landing or simply don't know if it is safe to sail, other members can help.
- ✪ The club will provide storage for your boat and changing facilities. Most clubs will also provide catering and organise off-the-water social events.
- ✪ The club will organise regular racing and sailing courses for its members. This is a great way to improve your sailing skills and to make friends.
- ✪ The club will provide reliable safety boat cover during events.

Below: **Most facilities have slipways and pontoons.**

Learn to sail on holiday

Beach club holidays with organised dinghy sailing provide great opportunities. You can learn to sail in a warm location with tuition from professionals. You can try a wide range of equipment, with a safety boat on hand. Be aware, though, that what different holiday operators offer can vary greatly. For instance, a specialist sailing company will provide top levels of equipment and tuition that is suitable for all standards. Beach club holidays, on the other hand, cater to a broader recreational market and are not likely to have the same choice of dinghy or catamaran sailing gear.

Warm weather and a relaxed atmosphere can give a great introduction to sailing. Dinghy sailing back home may be different and more challenging, with tidal waters and difficult weather, but you can rest assured it will be just as much fun.

Safety cover

Always sail with safety cover when you are learning (see p18), and, if possible, when you are experienced as well. Safety cover should be provided by a qualified safety boat driver who knows how to handle a rescue boat in close proximity to a dinghy, which may be capsized with crew in the water. Beware of rescue by a well-meaning but inexperienced motorboat driver: people who are experienced will be able to manage the propeller and the movement of their boat without inflicting injury.

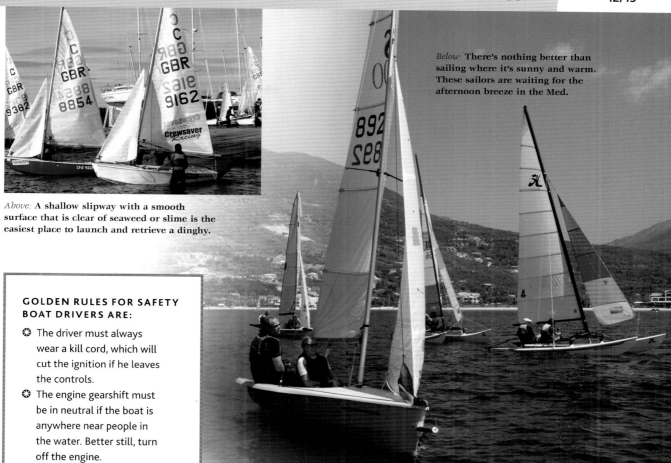

Below: **There's nothing better than sailing where it's sunny and warm. These sailors are waiting for the afternoon breeze in the Med.**

Above: **A shallow slipway with a smooth surface that is clear of seaweed or slime is the easiest place to launch and retrieve a dinghy.**

GOLDEN RULES FOR SAFETY BOAT DRIVERS ARE:

- ✪ The driver must always wear a kill cord, which will cut the ignition if he leaves the controls.
- ✪ The engine gearshift must be in neutral if the boat is anywhere near people in the water. Better still, turn off the engine.

Safety boat cover

You should find quality safety boat cover:

- ✪ On sailing holidays at beach clubs and similar operations.
- ✪ On a sailing course staged by a school, club or activities centre.
- ✪ During a regatta or organised sailing event.
- ✪ During organised racing by a sailing club.

Right: **Avoid sailing without safety cover – you never know when it might be useful!**

Inland and coastal sailing

You can sail a dinghy inland (such as on a lake or reservoir) or on the open sea. Sailing inland has the benefit of fresh water, but wind may be unpredictable. Sailing on the sea can provide unlimited space, but tide and waves make conditions more challenging.

Sailing on inland waters

Advantages:

✓ It is very pleasant to sail on clean, fresh water. It gives the boat and its equipment a free wash instead of leaving it covered in a sticky, salty residue.

✓ No sandy beach also means no sand in your boat or in your sailing equipment.

✓ A small lake or reservoir is comparatively safe, with a compact area for safety cover. If you get into trouble and can't make it back, your boat will be blown to the nearest leeward shore.

✓ The water level won't drop and rise due to tides, and there won't be tidal flow. (This isn't the case when sailing on a river, which may have a strong tidal flow and rise and fall.)

✓ Lakes and reservoirs used for sailing are often in beautiful areas. The English Lake District, Lake Garda and Lake Como in Italy and Canada's Lake Sharbot can provide great sailing as well as stunning scenery.

✓ With limited space, inland sailing locations are often excellent for tactical racing.

✓ If you live inland, the perfect stretch of inland water may be close to home.

Left: **A big advantage of inland water is that there is no tide. The water will be at the same level when you sail back to shore!**

Below: **Lake Garda is one of the world's great inland sailing venues, providing a huge area in a stunning location.**

Sailing on coastal waters

Advantages:

✓ There are no limits on how far you can sail, apart from common sense and practicality.

✓ There is also plenty of space without being hemmed in by other boats.

✓ Sailing in a harbour, bay or along the coast provides plenty of variety and interest.

✓ The challenge of tides will spice up your sailing.

✓ Open water with waves is very enjoyable for the more experienced, high-performance sailor.

✓ Sandy beaches can be beautiful places when you launch and land in a boat.

Below: **Salt spray can be corrosive, and so should be washed off your boat and out of your clothes when you come back to shore.**

Disadvantages:

✗ Sand and salt spray get in your boat and in your clothes.

✗ Tides can provide a major challenge. When there is a large tidal rise and fall, sailing access may be limited. If you get the timing wrong, there may be a very long way to drag your boat over sand or mud.

✗ Sea conditions will change with the tide. At high water, there may be tricky waves breaking on the beach. You may not be able to sail against strong tidal flow, which will sweep your boat in the wrong direction.

✗ An onshore wind will pile up waves on the beach, making it difficult to launch or land. An offshore wind can be dangerous: light and fluky inshore, but blowing hard offshore.

✗ Safety cover will be limited, unless you are sailing in a club event or you are with an organised group.

Disadvantages:

✗ You may run out of space. High-performance dinghies need large areas of water to perform on.

✗ Unless you are sailing well away from the lake shore, the wind will be affected by hills, trees, buildings and any other obstructions on the windward shore (where the wind is blowing from), which may create a gusty, shifty pattern.

✗ A small lake surrounded by trees will have rapid changes in wind speed and direction, but many sailors enjoy that for tactical racing.

✗ There may be a muddy shoreline where you launch. The water may not be perfectly clean, with the chance of there being algae and other growths.

✗ In winter, freshwater lakes and reservoirs can become very cold. Drysuits should be worn; capsize is best avoided – if possible!

TIP

Sailing on fresh water is cleaner but can be colder than salt water! Make sure you remember to wear suitable clothing.

Clothing

Sailing has a tendency to be a surprisingly chilly sport wherever you are and you need to make sure you dress for the weather. In addition, when you get wet, evaporation results in rapid cooling – wet skin loses heat 30 times faster than dry.

Personal buoyancy

Buoyancy aids are available in waistcoat or pull-on styles and should be a close fit that does not obstruct your upper body when sailing. If you capsize and are in the water, the buoyancy aid should stay secure around your body, without floating up over your head.

The main advantage of a lifejacket over a buoyancy aid is that all lifejackets are designed to float an unconscious person face-upwards in the water, whereas a buoyancy aid is simply a swimming aid. A lifejacket is therefore more appropriate for anyone who is not a particularly strong swimmer.

Choosing an effective wetsuit

How effective a wetsuit is at keeping you warm depends on several factors:

❂ A close fit that moulds to your body, preventing cold water washing around the inside, is vital. To achieve this, the material used (Neoprene) must be supple

Super-stretch panelling

3mm Neoprene construction

Reinforced knee panels

STEAMER

Side pockets

Neoprene waistband

HIKING SHORTS

Rubber neck

DRYTOP SMOCK

Adjustable strap

Moulded sole

DINGHY SHOES

and stretchy and cut specifically for a male or female fit. When trying on a wetsuit, make sure you can bend and stretch in any direction and that the neck is comfortable.

⚙ The thicker the Neoprene, the warmer and more constrictive it will be. Most wetsuits therefore combine thicker body panels with thinner leg and arm panels – maybe 5mm for the body and 3mm for arms and legs.

⚙ How waterproof? Neoprene is waterproof but a wetsuit cannot be fully watertight and the more cold water that flushes through the inside of the suit, the colder you will become. The best wetsuits have sealed stitching and a shaped, tight fit at the ankles (or thighs on shortie wetsuits), wrists (or arms on short-arm wetsuits) and neck. Full-length Neoprene flaps will reduce the amount of water the zip lets inside the suit.

A wetsuit with full-length legs and arms plus a back zip provides the best compromise for dinghy sailing – these are generally called steamers. A 'convertible' has removable Neoprene arms – a useful feature. A 'shortie' wetsuit is good for performance sailing in warmer weather, but leaves your knees unprotected. A wind- and waterproof dry top can be worn over the wetsuit, providing increased protection in colder weather. Make sure it is a loose fit so you can move easily.

A drysuit is a totally waterproof, loose-fitting one-piece suit and can be worn with thermal base and mid-layers – it's therefore a top choice for winter sailing.

Boots or shoes?

Dinghy boots should feature a tough and grippy moulded rubber sole combined with a Neoprene sock to protect your ankles. Dinghy shoes use the same Neoprene and rubber and are more comfortable in hot weather, but give no ankle protection.

Full protection

It is important to protect your extremities from the cold when sailing, so choose a good hat, gloves and footwear. Gloves need to protect your hands from the ravages of handling ropes – short-finger gloves with a reinforced palm are the best choice for dinghy sailing, enabling greater dexterity than full-finger gloves. You also need to protect your skin and eyes from the sun.

Trapeze harnesses

If the boat you sail has a trapeze, you will need a trapeze harness, which is worn over the wetsuit and under

Above: **Wind and water will cool you down, so always dress to stay warm!**

the buoyancy aid. The harness has a hook or spreader bar, which must be adjusted so that it is pulled in as close as possible to your body. Beware of using an older harness – it may not be of a type that readily releases you from the boat in the event of a capsize.

Below: **The trapeze harness is normally worn underneath the buoyancy aid. Sailing shoes are vital for good grip on the deck.**

Common-sense seamanship

Respect for the sea, or the inland waters on which you sail, is a key part of staying safe. Stick to these essential principles, make sure you understand the basic rules of the road and keep a constant lookout for other boats.

Tides and weather

Winds are stronger over water than on land and the weather can change quickly, even on apparently balmy days. Get an up-to-date weather forecast – a coastal waters one if sailing on the sea – before launching (see p140). In tidal waters you also need high and low water times, plus the direction and speed of tidal streams. This is especially important if tides will sweep you away from your launch site, or if 'wind against tide' conditions could kick up a rough sea. Beware of sailing too far downwind of your base – otherwise you'll have a slower, more tiring and colder sail back.

Clothing and lifejackets

Even if you stay dry, it's much colder afloat than on land, and if you get wet, body heat drains quickly away. Proper clothing suitable for all the conditions you may encounter is therefore essential (see p16). There's always a risk with dinghy sailing that you will end up in the water, so wear a well-fitting buoyancy aid or lifejacket at all times.

Safety cover

Ideally, when learning to sail, you shouldn't go out without a safety boat manned by a trained crew. On a sailing course, and during organised club activities, there will always

Above: **Stormy skies with wind building are no problem if there is safety cover close to hand.**

be one of these in attendance. If you do sail without backup, make sure you tell someone ashore so they can raise the alarm if you're late returning. You should also make sure you have ways to attract attention if you get into trouble, such as distress flares and a handheld VHF radio. It is good practice to always carry an anchor, paddle or oars, and a compass, too.

Stay with the boat!

If you have a problem always stay with the boat – it has enough buoyancy to stay afloat even if inverted or flooded, and is a large target that's easy for rescuers to find, unlike a person in the water.

Left: **Proper clothing suitable for all the conditions you may encounter is essential.**

Rules of the road

Remember who gives way

- A sailing boat on port tack gives way to one on starboard.
- Allow plenty of room when passing another boat.
- If two sailing boats are converging on the same tack, the leeward boat (sailing closer to the wind) has right of way.
- Sailing boats do not have right of way just because they are racing, but in some situations it may be courteous to give way to a racer.
- Power gives way to sail, but not if the motorboat is in a channel or constrained by its draught.
- There are also other classes of vessel to which sailing boats must give way, including those engaged in fishing and dredging.
- Make your intentions clear.
- An overtaking boat must keep clear of the vessel she is passing.
- It's the ultimate responsibility of all vessels to avoid a collision.

Buoys and channel markers

- Colour codings for deepwater channels vary in different parts of the world. In Europe, leave red (port) markers to the left and green (starboard) markers to the right when entering a channel. In the USA, leave red (port) markers to the right and green (starboard) markers to the left.
- Keep to the right-hand side of a channel at all times.
- As a dinghy sailor, it makes sense to stay out of a main channel in which large boats navigate. Don't get stuck in the wind shadow of a ferry.
- If there is tidal flow, it will be strongest in deep water and weakest in shallow water.

Right: **Starboard tack boat (foreground) has right of way over port tack boats when beating to windward. Get it right! You must know the rules.**

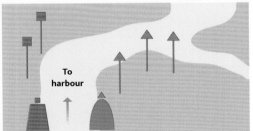
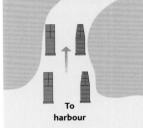

Above: **System A buoyage – when entering a harbour, the port-hand marker (red) is on the left and the starboard-hand marker (green) is on the right.**

In the USA the buoyage system (system B) is different from other parts of the world: port-hand buoys are green and starboard-hand buoys are red.

Right: **Keep out of the main channel – between the buoys – when entering or leaving a harbour. This will help you keep out of the way of bigger boats.**

Dealing with emergencies

It's essential to be fully prepared and equipped to deal with any emergency situation that you may face, and also to be able to call for help if necessary.

The huge range of dinghies and different ways in which they are used makes it impossible to be prescriptive for every situation that might be faced. However, as well as common-sense seamanship (see p18) there are a number of fundamentals that must be observed.

Those who race dinghies, whether inland or on the sea, should find that their class rules or the notice of race or sailing instructions for each event they compete in will specify exactly what they are required to carry. On a sailing course, and during organised club activities, there will always be a rescue boat in attendance, but experienced sailors who sail on coastal waters without the backup of organised rescue cover need to ensure they are properly prepared with the safety equipment outlined below. This will enable you to deal with common problems such as becoming becalmed and bailing water out of the boat following a capsize or swamping. If necessary, you will also be able to summon outside assistance from other boats or via the coastguard.

Essential safety equipment

Basic safety equipment includes an anchor, oars or a paddle – to get you back to shore in a calm, or in the event of gear failure – a bailer, appropriate clothing and lifejackets or buoyancy aids. You should also have a means of signalling distress, indicating that you need to be rescued. The classic way of doing

Above: **Marine flares are the best way of attracting attention. Use orange smoke for daytime and a red handheld at dusk or at night.**

this is with distress flares – these are typically orange smoke for daytime use, or a red handheld for inshore use at night – don't forget that if you're planning to sail in the late afternoon or evening, any problem that arises may delay you getting back to shore by which time it could be dark.

Below: **Sailing instructions or the notice of race will specify what kit you need to carry.**

Left: **On a sailing course, or during organised club activities, there will always be a rescue boat with appropriately trained crew on hand.**

Most flares burn for only 40 seconds, so it's usual to fire them in pairs – the second about half a minute after the first. A handheld marine VHF radio can be used to contact the Coastguard or another vessel directly – if necessary via a MAYDAY distress message. It's also important to share your sailing plans with someone ashore so they can raise the alarm if you're late returning.

Mobile phones have also been used successfully to raise the alarm from on board a boat, but it's important to recognise their weaknesses. They need a proper waterproof bag, battery life may be severely limited and, unlike a marine VHF radio, nearby vessels that may be able to assist won't hear your calls. A basic knowledge of first aid is also important for those who need to be self-sufficient when sailing.

Right: **It's important to practise capsize drills, so you know how to recover your dinghy afterwards.**

Entrapment

In the event of a capsize, there's a small risk of becoming trapped under the hull if it totally inverts, or under the trampoline of a catamaran. If trapped under the hull, there's usually a large air pocket that allows you to breathe with no problem, providing the trapeze harness releases from the trapeze wire – the modern types should automatically unhook in such a situation.

If trapped under a sail or under the trampoline, try to use your arms to push yourself out to open water. When sailing a catamaran, it's worth carrying a sharp knife to cut the trampoline if necessary.

Securing a tow

If you need to be towed, the towline may be subject to considerable loads, especially if several dinghies are towed at once. You should therefore secure the towline to the strongest point on the boat – this is most likely to be the mast step. Use a round turn and two half hitches, so the knot can be released under load.

Ropework

Ropes are used for different purposes on a boat and have different dimensions and qualities. The strength of rope depends on how it is made, its diameter and the material it is made from.

Different types of rope

All ropes, whether made from natural or synthetic materials, are made from strands of yarn, twisted or braided into finished rope.

1. Braided rope has a central core of strands protected by an outer cover. This creates a rope that offers the best compromise between strength, stretch resistance and lightness of weight. Braided rope is widely used for control lines, halyards and sheets. For some applications on performance dinghies the outer cover is omitted to save as much weight as possible.

2. Stranded or 'laid' rope is made with three or more polyester strands wound in a spiral. It is widely used for mooring lines and may also be used on some traditional-style dinghies, where aesthetics are judged to be more important than minimising stretch.

Above: **Braided rope is secured around a horn cleat on a pontoon. Note how the rope is wrapped around the base of the cleat and then over the horns.**

Common materials for dinghy ropes include pre-stretched polyester and high-tech yarns such as Dyneema. Kevlar and Spectra were also extensively used in the past, but have largely been superseded by Dyneema.

Below: **To uncleat a rope from a jamming cleat, pull it upwards and towards you.**

Coiling rope

1. Pull out an equal length of rope for each coil. Use your thumb and forefinger to twist the top to ensure each coil hangs straight.
2. Leave enough rope to take several turns around the main body of coils.
3. Pull a loop through the top hole in the coils.
4. Pull the loop down over the coils.
5. Tighten the free end. The coiled rope is secure and ready for storage or use.

Securing rope

Butterfly cleats: The butterfly cleat provides the simplest solution to holding a rope under load. To secure the rope, take a turn around the base of the cleat. After the first full turn, continue with one or more figure-of-eight loops, followed by another round turn.

Jamming cleats: These are used for many controls on dinghies. The rope is cleated by pulling it through the jaws with downward pressure and released by pulling it a little towards you and upwards.

Jamming cleats are often provided for sheets as holding them under tension for extended periods can be tiring. However, it's important to keep a hand on the line so that it can be released instantly to depower the rig in a strong gust of wind. Anyone who is not familiar with using jamming cleats should practise releasing the sheet when it's under load before needing to do so in anger.

Secure the bundle of coils by taking three turns round the top part with the end of the rope. Push a loop through the middle of the coils and turn it over the top of the coil before tightening the free end.

Rope sense

If a rope is under load, make sure it is secure. Beware of grabbing a rope that is running free; a towline for instance may come under considerable load if a number of dinghies are being towed. A rope under load creates friction, which can 'burn' the unprotected palm of your hand.

Rope will fray due to being constantly pulled through a fairlead or block. The outer casing will become damaged or a strand may start to fail. Ropes should be regularly checked for wear and chafe, and replaced if damaged.

Synthetic rope should be heat-sealed, ideally by cutting it with a 'hot knife' which is available from chandlers, to ensure that the end of the rope cannot unravel or separate from its cover.

Above: **An unused rope is best stored in a neat coil as this will prevent it becoming tangled with other lines.**

Coiling rope

It's important to always keep things tidy on board. Rope should be coiled to form a neat bundle of loops, which can be uncoiled and used in seconds. If you leave loose rope in an untidy bundle, it will almost certainly tangle and snag.

To coil a rope, make clockwise loops with one hand and hold the coils with the other hand. Make sure each loop is the same size by paying out an even length of rope for each coil. Due to its construction, rope tends to twist when coiled.

You can overcome this by twisting the rope between thumb and forefinger as you make the loop. Some rope – especially long lengths of anchor warp – is most easily coiled in figure-of-eight loops.

Below: **Securing a towline – a round turn and two half hitches is the best knot to use as it can be released under load. Slide it down the mast to deck level.**

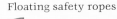
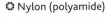

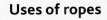

Uses of ropes

✪ Nylon (polyamide)	Anchoring, mooring, permanent moorings and towing
✪ Polyester (Terylene, Dacron)	Anchor warps and mooring lines
✪ Polypropylene	Floating safety ropes
✪ Spectra, Dyneema, Kevlar	Halyards, sheets, guys and other sail controls

Elementary lessons & core skills

The 360-degree sailing circle

Sailing allows you to harness the free power of the wind to make progress in any direction. A dinghy can even sail close to the direction the wind is blowing from, unlike the old square-riggers, which could only sail where the wind would take them.

Sailing towards the wind

Sailing as close as possible towards the wind is known as 'beating to windward'. Despite centuries of development, a sailboat cannot and never will be able to sail directly into the wind.

The type of boat and its rig will determine how close it can really sail towards the wind. Beating to windward at an angle of about 35 degrees to the wind direction is the closest a racing dinghy is likely to get in ideal conditions, but the angle may be greater than 45 degrees for a traditional dayboat.

The zone in which it's impossible to sail is called the 'no-go zone'. The only way you can sail through this is by 'tacking': changing direction by turning the bow through the wind so that the wind blows on the other side of the sails. A series of tacks will eventually lead you to a point that is directly upwind.

Reaching across the wind

If you turn the bow further away from the wind, so that the breeze is blowing more on to the side of the boat, this is called 'bearing away'.

When the wind is coming from the side of the boat, this is called 'reaching'. This may be a 'close reach' with the wind blowing slightly from in front, a 'beam reach' with the wind blowing directly from the side, or a 'broad reach' with the wind blowing slightly from behind.

Reaching is generally the fastest and most enjoyable point of sailing for all boats, with the wind direction allowing the boat to be driven at maximum speed and comfort.

Sailing with the wind

If you turn the bow even further away from the wind (bear away), so that the wind is blowing from behind the boat, you are 'running'. If the wind is directly behind the boat, you are 'running dead downwind'.

Contrary to what you might expect, this is often not a particularly enjoyable way to sail. The wind is only blowing on to the windward side of the sail, pushing it along like an old square-rigged sailing ship. Without an extra downwind sail, known as a 'spinnaker' (a large lightweight sail), the boat will feel quite slow as it is not well powered by the wind.

It may also feel unstable, because it is a lot more difficult to maintain balance and prevent rolling with the wind blowing from behind, particularly if there are waves.

Beware of gybes

If you bear away too far from the wind, it will start blowing from the same side the mainsail is on – this is said to be 'running by the lee'. Be careful as if the wind gets behind the mainsail it will slam the boom over in a crash gybe. Always ensure that when you gybe it is intentional, and everyone is aware. In a safe gybe, the swing of the mainsail across the boat is carefully controlled (see p38).

Left: **Changing direction always means resetting the sails to suit the new wind angle relative to the boat.**

Points of sailing

Sails are controlled by ropes known as 'sheets'. They are pulled in tight when sailing close to the wind, eased out when sailing across the wind, and eased all the way out when sailing with the wind behind. The transition from beat to beat is a *tack*; the transition from run to run is a *gybe*.

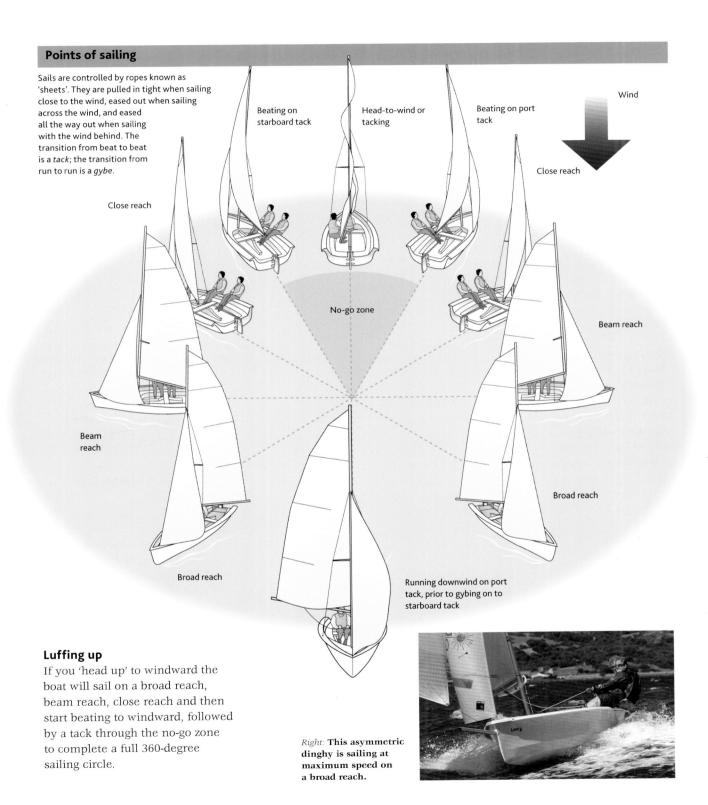

Beating on starboard tack

Head-to-wind or tacking

Beating on port tack

Wind

Close reach

Close reach

Close reach

No-go zone

Beam reach

Beam reach

Beam reach

Broad reach

Broad reach

Broad reach

Running downwind on port tack, prior to gybing on to starboard tack

Luffing up

If you 'head up' to windward the boat will sail on a broad reach, beam reach, close reach and then start beating to windward, followed by a tack through the no-go zone to complete a full 360-degree sailing circle.

Right: **This asymmetric dinghy is sailing at maximum speed on a broad reach.**

Sailing on a reach

Start sailing in light winds up to a maximum of force 3, using a stable, easily handled dinghy. Begin by sailing on a reaching course, with the wind blowing across the boat.

Wind on the beam

A beam reach, with wind blowing at 90 degrees across the boat, provides stable and efficient sailing. The wind produces maximum airflow on both sides of the sails, which can be balanced by the crew leaning out to windward. Power from the sails, plus lift from the centreboard or daggerboard, drives the boat forwards instead of sideways, which reduces heel and enables the boat to sail at a good speed but with minimal effort.

Steering the boat

The helm normally sits on the windward side of the boat, facing the sails, with the crew doing most of the task of balancing the boat. Pushing the tiller away from you will turn the boat up towards the wind, while pulling it towards you will turn the boat away from the wind. It will very quickly become second

Right: **Keep the boat flat when sailing on a reach by hiking out or easing the mainsheet. If the boat is flat it is faster and it will be easier to steer, with less weather helm.**

nature. Most dinghies have tiller extensions that enable the helm to hike out when necessary to balance the boat – try to get accustomed to using this from the outset.

Basic sail adjustment

Simply pull the mainsheet and jib sheet in just far enough to stop the sails flapping. But resist the temptation to over-sheet – this stalls the airflow across the sails, reduces forward drive and increases heel.

Fore-and-aft trim

The boat must be kept upright, but also trimmed fore-and-aft (longitudinally) for best performance and ease of handling. In lighter winds, keep weight forward to lift the stern and thereby reduce drag, which will slow the boat. As the wind increases and the boat accelerates, move weight back. When sailing double-handed, both crew should sit as close together as possible.

Keep upright

Try to sail the boat as upright as possible. When a gust hits, ease the sheets or hike out to avoid the boat heeling. If the boat heels too far:

❂ It will sail slower, due to the side of the hull dragging in the water.
❂ It will slide sideways, due to the daggerboard or centreboard providing less resistance.

Left: **Perfect trim, both sideways and fore and aft. The crew of this National 12 demonstrate how a dinghy should be sailed.**

✪ It will develop weather helm – you'll need to pull the tiller towards you continuously to maintain a straight course – as the rudder blade loses contact with the water.

✪ It will be a struggle for the crew to control the boat while hanging over the side.

How to hike

Hiking or sitting out is a major feature of dinghy sailing. Your weight provides a counterbalance to the wind in the sails tipping the boat. Sit on the sidedeck and put your feet under the toe straps, with the tips of your boots sticking out the other side. Modern dinghies have good ergonomics that allow you to slide in or out over the side. When the boat heels, drop your body over the side of the boat – the toe straps will ensure that you are secure.

How comfortable it is to hike will depend on your fitness and strength, as well as leg reach from the side of the boat to the toe straps. If you intend to race you will need to take hiking seriously; the more you lean out in a breeze, the faster the boat will go! Hard-wearing hiking shorts are recommended to make this more comfortable.

The joy of planing

In force 3–4 winds and above the boat should start planing, with the hull leaving its stern wave behind and powering along at speed on top of the bow wave. The crew must move back to lift the bow, but if the boat drops off the plane (slowing down with the bow dropping) the crew should move forward again.

Above: **Watch the sail and watch your course. If the tiller starts pulling, ease off the mainsheet. The crew of this boat are enjoying a relaxed and fun ride, reaching with the wind on the beam.**

Below: **Sailing on a well-powered reach is physical. The best sailors really work the boat by constantly moving their bodyweight in and out, fore and aft.**

Above: **Bows flying, crew aft and planing fast. This singlehander has a good dose of speed on a reach.**

How to tack

If you want to sail towards where the wind is blowing from, you will need to change tack. Fluid and fast tacking is a vital element of dinghy sailing. The tacking manoeuvre is relatively easy, but a perfect tack relies on knowing how to change over hands.

Turning the boat

The technique required for tacking a dinghy is straightforward, with the boat turning from tack to tack through an angle of about 60 degrees.

- Sail to windward with the sails sheeted in.
- Push the tiller away, making the boat spin around on its centreboard or daggerboard.
- As the bow passes through the eye of the wind (when it is 'head-to-wind') the crew moves across the cockpit to the new windward side. The jib sheet must be let off so that it will run free, with the mainsheet uncleated and eased.
- The helm straightens out the rudder as the boat bears away on the new course, and sheets in the mainsail at the same time.
- The crew sheets in the jib. Both crew lean out on the new windward side to counteract heeling.

Handling tiller and mainsheet

Most modern dinghies have a centre mainsheet; the lead of the sheet is in the middle of the boat, just forward of the helm who holds the sheet with his leading hand. Good technique is required to change hands during a tack, while keeping control of the tiller and mainsheet throughout the manoeuvre. The length of the tiller extension will help determine how it is achieved: practice will make perfect, so keep trying!

- Hold the tiller extension across the front of your body, using a 'dagger' grip with your back hand.

- Uncleat the mainsheet to ease the mainsail as you push the tiller away to steer into the tack.
- Pivot your body through 180 degrees, facing forwards, as you cross the cockpit. As you do this, keep hold of the mainsheet in your front hand and continue to steer the boat round with your back hand.
- Let your 'dagger' grip twist round the tiller extension as you move to the new side, swivelling the tiller extension forwards so that it doesn't hit the boom, which will be in the middle of the boat.
- Twist your body round to sit up on the new sidedeck, still holding the tiller extension – which is now behind your back – with the same hand. The other hand is still holding the mainsheet.
- Move the mainsheet hand across your body so that you can grasp the lower half of the tiller extension. This now becomes your back hand holding the tiller extension. For a moment you will hold both the tiller extension and

Right: **1. To start the tack, steer the boat up into the wind. 2. If the wind is light, rolling it to windward will make the tack more dynamic, turning the boat quickly and powering up the mainsail on the new side. Note how the helmsman has flipped the tiller extension under the boom, just before he moves to the new side. The crew lets the jib backwind to help pull the bow round. 3. The helm pivots across the boat facing forward, then sits on the side, with the tiller extension held behind his back. When the boat has settled down, he changes his front and back hands.**

Tacking a centre mainsheet boat

the mainsheet in the same hand, before flicking the tiller extension past your back shoulder and across your body, and grabbing the mainsheet with your new front hand.

Transom mainsheet

Many classic dinghy classes are fitted with a mainsheet led from the transom. If you tack with a transom-led mainsheet, you will need to pivot through 180 degrees, facing towards the stern as you change sides. The obvious disadvantage is that you can't watch where the boat is heading!

Below: **Perfect tiller extension control, as the helm of a Merlin Rocket walks through a tack.**

Tacking a transom (aft) mainsheet boat

1. The crew of this Enterprise are sailing at good speed going into the tack. 2. The helmsman steers into the wind, while the crew keeps the jib sheeted in to pull the bow round. 3. The helm pivots facing backwards, while moving across the boat as the crew sheets in the jib on the new side.

How to tack (2)

What happens if the boat stops as the bow turns into the wind and won't keep turning on to the new tack? Keep practising, don't get 'stuck in irons', and before long you will be a master at powered-up roll tacks!

Left: **Note how the jib is still sheeted as this RS200 tacks, helping to pull the bow through the eye of the wind without stalling.**

Stuck in irons – with jib

If you steer the boat into a tack and it stops head-to-wind, you are 'stuck in irons'. The boat will sit still, and then start to drift backwards. Keep the jib sheeted in on the old side until the bow has swung through the eye of the wind, and only then let go to sheet in on the new side.

If you have already let go of the jib sheet and the boat stops head-to-wind, 'back' the jib by pulling in on the old side so that the wind can blow against it and blow the bow round.

A dinghy without a jib is more prone to getting stuck in irons. Make sure you have plenty of 'way on' as you turn into the tack. The boat should be up to speed and not about to stall, so the momentum will help carry it through the turn.

Push-push, pull-pull (no jib)

If you get stuck in irons on a singlehanded boat such as a Pico, Topper or Laser:

✪ Push the boom and tiller away at the same time. Pushing the boom will backwind the sail so that it fills on the other side and drives the boat backwards; pushing the tiller will allow the boat to reverse, so that it turns away from head-to-wind.

✪ Pull the tiller and pull in the sail. Pulling the tiller will help the boat bear away on the tack; pulling in the sheet will power the sail to drive the boat forwards.

Roll tacks

In lighter winds, a technique known as 'roll tacking' can produce a quicker and more powerful turn. Instead of relying on the rudder, an aggressive change of crew weight plays the major role in spinning the boat through the turn. The rolling action powers up the sails and provides faster acceleration on the new tack.

✪ Steer gently into the tack, with the boat heeling to leeward (away from the wind), which will make it want to turn towards the wind.

✪ Stay on the windward side and roll the boat into the turn as the boom crosses the centreline.

✪ Ease the mainsheet and move quickly on to the new windward sidedeck, with the new leeward side heeling right over as the boat points in the new direction.

✪ Lean out and sheet in the sails in one dynamic movement, bringing the boat upright and powering it up at the same time.

Below: **The roll tack is a dynamic movement that rolls the boat through the tack. Note how the helm will be holding the tiller extension in his new front hand when he sits on the side, ready for the changeover between the tiller and sheet hands.**

How to tack a catamaran

Catamarans tend to tack slowly, due to the drag from one hull pivoting round the outside of the turn. High-performance cats with daggerboards tend to tack quite easily; recreational cats with skegs or asymmetric hulls may get stuck head-to-wind if you don't use the right technique.

- The cat should be sailing at speed before the helm steers into the tack with the mainsheet in. Don't ease it out yet.
- Steer carefully. The two rudders will act like a brake if you slam them over too fast.
- Keep the jib sheeted in.
- Stay on the windward side of the boat until the jib has backed, with the wind blowing on the other side, which will push the bows through the tack.
- Keep the jib sheeted on the old side until the cat is correctly lined up for the new tack at about 40 degrees to the wind.
- The helm must steer carefully through the tack, pivoting to face backwards while moving to the new side of the boat.
- While moving across the boat, ease the mainsheet by about 30cm to loosen the mainsail and allow the full-length battens to pop on to the new side.
- Bear away carefully as the crew sheets in the jib on the new tack, pulling in the mainsheet as the cat accelerates back to full speed.

Tacking in a catamaran

1. Note how the helm is kneeling on the side ready to tack – this is a good cat sailor's position as he pushes the tiller away.

2. Always ease off the mainsheet as you go through the tack on a cat, or the boat may stall head-to-wind.

3. The helm pivots round, facing aft, on to the new windward side, before bearing away on the new tack.

4. Straighten out the course and sheet in carefully to allow the cat to accelerate smoothly on the new tack.

Sailing into the wind

If you want to head in the direction from which the wind is blowing, you need to sail the boat as close to the true wind as possible. For novices, beating to windward efficiently can be the most challenging point of sail.

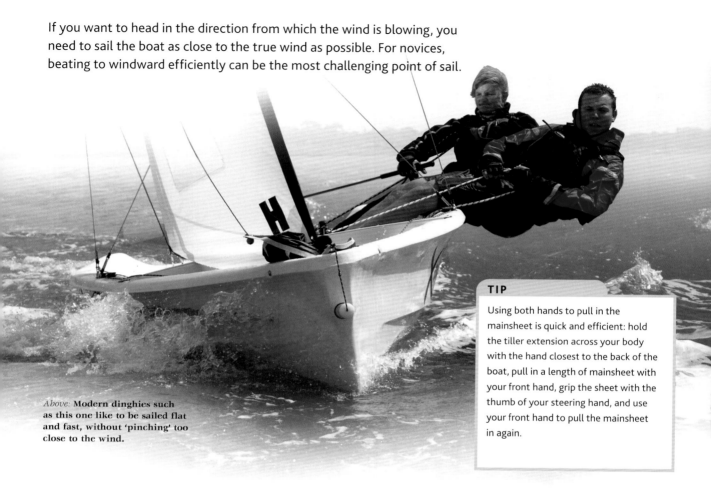

Above: **Modern dinghies such as this one like to be sailed flat and fast, without 'pinching' too close to the wind.**

TIP

Using both hands to pull in the mainsheet is quick and efficient: hold the tiller extension across your body with the hand closest to the back of the boat, pull in a length of mainsheet with your front hand, grip the sheet with the thumb of your steering hand, and use your front hand to pull the mainsheet in again.

Wind from ahead

You can't sail directly into the wind (this is the 'no go zone') but you can sail towards the wind with a series of zigzags. Depending on the boat, skill of the crew and sea conditions, it's possible to sail at an angle of 35–45 degrees to the true wind.

Wind blowing from ahead flows over both sides of the sails, which provides forward drive, aided by the dynamic lift and lateral resistance of the daggerboard or centreboard. Resist the tendency of the boat to heel, by hiking out and depowering the mainsail if necessary – dinghies sail better if they are kept upright.

In very light winds both the mainsheet and jib sheet should be pulled in, but not too taut. As the wind increases, the mainsheet and jib sheet should be pulled in firmly, then steer a course so that the telltales (short strips of cloth or wool attached near the leading edge on both sides of the sail) are horizontal.

For best performance, holding the sheets is recommended, but for learning or leisure sailing, it is much less tiring to lock the sheets in their jamming cleats.

The jib sheet can generally be left cleated when a gust hits, but the helm will need to uncleat the

mainsheet with a quick upwards flick to ease the sheet. Practise pulling the mainsheet through the jamming cleat: pull the mainsheet slightly in and downwards to lock the sheet, pull it slightly in and upwards to unlock and let go.

Trim and heel

Keep weight well forward when sailing upwind, pushing down the bow and lifting the stern.

If a gust hits, you have two choices. Either ease the mainsheet to lose power and let the boat come upright, or 'luff' by steering a little towards the wind. The closer you

Above: **In light winds, you need to sit still and concentrate on keeping the boat moving upwind.**

Velocity made good (VMG)

Two boats wish to sail to a spot around 11 miles away and directly upwind. They will have to tack, beating to windward in a zigzag course, to arrive there. Boat A points at 30 degrees to the wind and sails at an average speed of 4 knots. Boat B points at 40 degrees to the wind and sails at an average speed of 7 knots.

Boat A has a VMG of 3.5 knots and Boat B has a VMG of 5.6 knots towards the windward mark. Boat B should reach the spot first thanks to better VMG. It takes about an hour longer for Boat A to get to the mark.

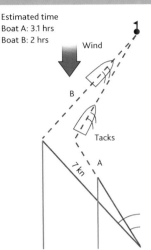

Estimated time
Boat A: 3.1 hrs
Boat B: 2 hrs

Wind

B

Tacks

7 Kn

A

The number and timing of the tacks each crew chooses to do is key to successfully meeting a mark. Every boat has an optimum angle to the wind. Find your own boat's optimum angle of performance and practise sailing! It may vary depending on the strength of the wind and other factors such as the tide.

sail towards the wind, the less heeling effect it will have on the sails. However, with less sail power, the boat will slow down.

Pointing high and low

Pointing very high with the sails backing is known as 'pinching to windward'. It can work well with traditional dinghy designs with narrow-bottomed hulls in the final approach to a racing mark, but never for long distances. Pinching does not work on modern skiff-style designs with flat-bottomed hulls, which need to be sailed fast at a greater angle to the wind: if you attempt to pinch, you will slow right down.

Catamarans

When sailing to windward in a catamaran, sheet in hard, with the mainsheet traveller on the centreline. Always sail free and fast, and go for VMG (see above). In a force 2–3, the windward hull will begin to lift off the water. Sailing a cat is quickest with the hull just 'kissing' the water. Flying the hull high may feel good, but will slow you down. If you can't hold the hull down, pull hard on the downhaul to depower the sail.

TIP

On a dinghy, you steer with the tiller extension. Hold the tiller extension with a downwards grip like a dagger! This will enable you to hold the end of the tiller extension across your body.

Right: **Don't let the boat heel too far, or it will slip sideways instead of making good progress upwind. On some dinghies, it might help to put a reef in the mainsail.**

Sailing away from the wind

If you want to head in the direction to which the wind is blowing, you need to sail with the wind behind. It sounds easiest to run straight downwind, but it may be better to follow a broad-reaching course.

Running dead downwind

Sailing with the wind directly behind can pose problems:

- The wind can't flow over both sides of the sail – it just pushes the boat along, with decreased sail efficiency.
- There is no side-on stability so the boat may start rolling. The crew of a double-handed dinghy can reduce this with one person sitting on the windward side and the other to leeward. A singlehander may need to crouch in the middle of the cockpit to balance the boat.
- If you don't steer the boat accurately when running there's a danger it will gybe, with the wind catching the mainsail on the wrong side and the boom slamming across. This is a common cause of capsize in strong winds.

- On a double-handed dinghy, the mainsail will blanket the jib. This can be cured by sheeting the jib on the windward side (known as 'goosewinging').
- However, goosewinging only works well if you sail a little by the lee, with the wind blowing over the leeward side of the stern – the same side as the mainsail.

Sail adjustment

On a double-handed boat the mainsheet should be let out until the boom is next to the leeward shroud. On a singlehanded dinghy it should be let out to a similar angle – around 80 degrees from the centreline.

Above: **Beware of the boat rolling to windward when you sail deep downwind. Pull in the mainsheet or push the tiller away to counteract this.**

Below: **The wind is blowing over the stern, with the boat heading a few degrees off sailing directly downwind. If the helmsman bears away any further, the mainsail will blanket the jib.**

The vang (kicking strap) should be sufficiently tight that the upper part of the mainsail does not twist forward of the rig. Failure to do this in a strong wind increases the tendency of the boat to roll.

Trim downwind

In light winds keep weight forward to ensure the stern doesn't drag. Move aft if the boat starts to sail fast.

Benefits of a broad reach

If you don't like the idea of rolling downwind, or experiencing an unexpected gybe, there's a simple solution: luff up towards the wind.

Steer on a broad reach with the wind blowing across the windward side of the stern. This powers up the jib on the leeward side and gives side-on stability that will stop rolling from occurring. You will need to sail a zigzag course with a series of broad reaches.

Modern dinghies with asymmetric spinnakers have much better velocity made good (VMG) if they are sailed this way, covering a greater distance but arriving sooner due to better speed. Sheet in the sails so that telltales are streaming horizontally and the boat is sailing well. A dinghy should plane easily on a broad reach. Be ready to move weight back to keep the bow flying. Sailing on a very broad reach may not provide a lot of side-on stability; beware of the boat rolling to windward in a lull.

Above: **Running dead downwind in a moderate wind. The helm kneels in the cockpit to balance the boat.**

Catamarans

Never sail directly downwind on a catamaran – drag from the two hulls, plus reduced airflow over the sails, makes this slow. Instead, sail on a series of reaches, with the wind blowing across the boat to increase the apparent wind. In a force 3 and above, steering towards the wind builds power, lifts the windward hull and enables the boat to accelerate.

As it does so, the apparent wind moves further ahead, which allows you to bear away on to more of a true downwind course. Beware of the leeward bow diving under the water at speed – move weight back so that both crew are by the rear beam.

> **TIP**
>
> If the boat starts rolling, pull the mainsheet to put some power into the sail, or steer a course that is closer to the wind.

Right: **When the mainsheet is eased, the boom is held down by a vang or gnav (see p48).**

How to gybe

Gybing a dinghy is changing tack with the wind blowing from behind instead of ahead. The mainsail is powered up throughout the turn, making it vital to keep the boat under full control. In stronger winds, it can be a difficult manoeuvre: making a mistake often leads to a capsize.

Scared of gybing?

People worry about gybing. During a tack, the boat turns into the wind and loses virtually all power in its sails, so it is fairly easy to maintain control. During a gybe, the boat turns away from the wind with the result that the sails are powered up all the time.

Gybing in light winds is easy, but in stronger winds a gybe becomes more dynamic. The boat sails through the turn at speed, and when the boat gybes the boom sweeps across the cockpit like a scythe. It is easy to lose control and capsize the dinghy.

Turning the boat

You may be sailing on a run or on a broad reach. You must:

- Steer precisely through the turn.
- When the wind direction changes from directly behind to blowing on the new windward side, help the mainsail to gybe by pulling the boom across.
- Straighten up on the new tack, while the boat is still sailing on a downwind course.

Gybing

- Prepare for the gybe. If you are sailing double-handed, make sure the crew is ready and knows what will happen.
- Pull the tiller to bear away into the gybe, with the mainsheet eased. Heel the boat to windward as this will help it to turn in lighter winds.
- The helm pivots to face forwards in the cockpit, swivelling the tiller extension to ensure that the rudder will steer the boat through a smooth arc.
- With the wind blowing from directly behind, the helm grabs the mainsheet as it falls off the boom.

Below: **With the gybe successfully accomplished, sheet in the mainsail and then power up on a new broad reach.**

- Just as the wind swings to the new windward side, the helm gives a sharp tug on the falls of the mainsheet. This should be enough to flick the boom and mainsail across the cockpit to the new side. Both crew duck under the boom as it swings across at speed.
- As the boom swings across, the helm changes sides, swivelling the tiller extension to keep steering in a smooth arc, while holding the mainsheet with his front hand.
- The helm pivots to sit on the new windward side, using the same hand technique as a tack. Sit well forward with the extension held behind your back, grab the lower half of the extension with your old sheet hand, flick the extension across the front of your body and grab the mainsheet with your new front hand.
- If you are sailing double-handed, the crew should change position by moving into the cockpit during the gybe. Let off the old jib sheet and pull it in on the new side as the boom swings across the cockpit. Move your weight to balance the boat and prevent it tipping over when the sails power up on the new tack.

TIP

The boom can swing across the cockpit at high speed. Don't get hit on the head! Beware of accidental gybes! The crew should take care not to get caught by the kicking strap: keep well behind it, but keep clear of the mainsheet at the same time.

Gybing a catamaran

It is easier to gybe a catamaran than a dinghy, because you have a much more stable platform with two hulls, and the multihull's speed downwind reduces the apparent wind strength. The technique is similar, with the main exception that the mainsheet is mounted on the rear beam.

- The helm steers into the gybe.
- As the wind swings behind, the helm pivots to face aft and kneels by the middle of the rear beam.
- The helm grabs the falls of the mainsheet to swing the mainsail to the new side.
- The helm keeps steering carefully through the arc of the turn, before straightening out the course as soon as the mainsail has gybed.

Gybing a singlehander

1. You can let the boat heel slightly to windward going into the gybe, which will help the hull carve round.

2. Duck as the boom comes across and straighten the course to keep sailing downwind with the boat held flat.

3. Don't let the boat round up onto a reach or heel to leeward, as this will often lead to a capsize.

How to gybe (2)

Why do dinghy sailors capsize when they gybe? Normally it is caused by lack of control. Work out what the problems are and you won't make any mistakes in the future.

Boom control

Decide when the moment is right to grab the falls of the mainsheet, then give a tug and send the boom on its journey across the cockpit. If you leave the boom to move on its own, it will wait until the boat has turned far enough for the wind to hit the back of the mainsail. The result is that the boom will swing over, violently and hard.

This may be dangerous for the crew (one good reason to sail wearing a helmet) and the momentum as the boom crashes across to the new side can cause the boat to tip right over. The helm may lose control of the steering, and the boat will keep turning on to a beam reach. With wind on the beam, the boat will capsize.

Don't turn too far

Keep control by gybing through the smallest possible angle. You only need to turn the boat through an arc that's big enough to gybe the mainsail on to the new tack. From there you can choose your direction: either keep sailing downwind, or head up on to a reach.

In light winds, it is possible to gybe through 180 degrees (from a beam reach to a beam reach) without much trouble. But as the wind gets stronger, letting the boat turn too far is asking for a capsize. Lack of steering control is the usual problem. The helm makes a mess of swinging the boom across the cockpit, so it crashes to the new side. In the heat of the moment he or she forgets how quickly the boat is turning and lets it spin right round until the bow is almost into the wind on the new tack, with the wind blowing the rig and boat over.

Don't trip

Some dinghies tend to trip on their centreboard or daggerboard as they gybe, which makes the boat heel over. On traditional dinghy classes, it's normal to gybe from run to run with the centreboard partly or fully retracted.

On singlehanded dinghies such as the Laser, it's normal to gybe with the daggerboard pulled up halfway. Make sure the top of the daggerboard is clear of the boom and kicking strap. On modern dinghies with asymmetric spinnakers, it's normal to leave the centreboard or daggerboard fully down.

> **TIP**
>
> Always grab the 'falls' of the mainsail (the two or three strands of rope that drop from the blocks on the boom) to pull the boom across. Hold them all together, so that you are giving the boom a highly effective tug.

Below left: **The disadvantage of gybing or tacking with a transom (aft) mainsheet is obvious – the helm can't see where the boat is going during the few seconds it takes to turn the boat.**

Below: **Gybing an Enterprise with a traditional transom (aft) mainsheet. The helm has to face aft, as the crew pulls on the kicking strap to help flick the boom across.**

Above: **Keep control of the rudder: straighten out your course as soon as the mainsail has gybed.**

Don't slow down

If you are sailing fast in a strong wind, try not to let the boat slow down when you gybe. The faster you sail through the gybe, the lighter the apparent wind will be, which makes it easier to keep control.

TIP

Steer from sailing deep downwind on one tack so that you are sailing deep downwind on the other tack. Keep the angle of the gybe tight and then adjust your course.

Left: **Stay low and concentrate on steering through the gybe, ready to flick the boom across at the precise moment when the stern switches through the eye of the wind.**

Sailing manoeuvres

Learning the basic manoeuvres for turning the boat and changing its direction is based on good wind awareness. Practise the manoeuvres in fine conditions, to get to know the feel of the boat and to be in control.

Above: **When gybing, the helm bears away by pulling the tiller. To maintain control, it is important to keep the boat flat.**

Heading up

'Heading up' is steering towards the wind. If sailing on a beam reach, with the wind blowing from the side, push the tiller away. The boat will start to turn towards the wind. You will find yourself at a different angle to the wind, so pull in the mainsheet to keep power in the sail.

Let the boat head up slowly until it is pointing at about 45 degrees to the wind. Straighten your course by centralising the rudder. Make a final adjustment of sail trim to ensure telltales are horizontal on both sides.

To sail closer to the wind, head up until the windward telltales begin lifting with the mainsheet pulled tight in. That is as close as you can sail to the wind – or the boat will stall.

To keep sailing properly, pull the tiller towards you until the windward telltales are horizontal once again.

Tacking

Tacking is steering the bows of the boat through the wind blowing directly from ahead. The boat must be powered up and moving as you steer into the tack. If not, it may get stuck head-to-wind 'in irons' and begin drifting backwards.

Gybing

Gybing is steering the stern of the boat through a wind blowing directly from behind. Unlike a tack, the sails will be powered up throughout the turn, which can make gybing quite tricky in stronger winds.

Bearing away

Bearing away means sailing away from the wind. Sailing on a beam reach, with the wind blowing from the side, pull the tiller towards your body.

Below: **When you need to tack, the helm steers into the wind by pushing the tiller away.**

Below: **The helmsman steers with the tiller and handles the mainsheet, while the crew controls the jib.**

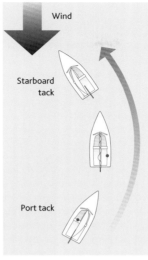

Above: **When tacking, the boat turns head-to-wind, then bears away to start sailing in the new direction. In this diagram, the boat has changed from port to starboard tack.**

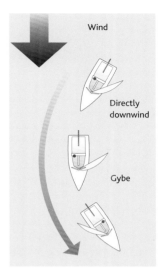

Above: **Bearing away downwind. The boom will swing across (gybe) as the stern changes its angle to the wind.**

The boat will start to turn away from the wind. You will need to let out the mainsheet to allow the boat to turn: if the mainsheet remains sheeted in, wind pressure will tend to tip the boat over instead of allowing it to bear away.

Let the boat bear away slowly until it is pointing at about 135 degrees to the wind, on a broad-reaching course. Straighten out by centralising the rudder.

You can bear away until the wind is blowing directly from behind the boat, which is now on a dead run. The sails should be let out to the maximum. Telltales will have no effect, since there is little or no windflow over the leeward side of the sail.

To avoid the possibility of an inadvertent gybe, head up a little so that the wind is blowing over the stern from the windward side.

The five essentials

These are the key considerations to have constantly in mind when sailing a dinghy:

- **Course made good**: Are you making good progress in the right direction? It's easy to become distracted from the optimum heading towards your destination or relative to the wind.
- **Balance**: Are you keeping the boat flat, or is it heeling either to windward or leeward and sailing inefficiently? If the boat is allowed to heel excessively you may even be in danger of a capsize.
- **Sail setting**: Are the sails set properly for the conditions and the wind direction? A common mistake is to sail with the sheets too tight, especially on a reach or a run. This is inefficient and increases heel, which makes controlling the boat harder.
- **Trim**: Is the fore-and-aft trim of the boat correct? In light winds, move your weight forward to reduce drag by lifting the relatively wide stern clear of the water. As the wind increases, move aft a little to level the boat in the fore-and-aft plane. When sailing away from the wind in a strong breeze, weight should be right back to keep the bows upwards, enabling the boat to plane fast with good control.
- **Daggerboard/centreboard position**: When sailing against the wind the board should be fully lowered to prevent the wind pushing the boat sideways. On a beam reach sheets are eased, there's less sideways force and the board can be lifted halfway. On a run, with the wind right behind, the board can be almost right up. This reduces drag and the risk of the boat 'tripping over' the board and capsizing.

Sail trim

Trimming the sails to the correct angle to the wind is an essential skill, which comes with practice. With a little experience you begin to get the feel of the boat in different types of weather conditions.

Above: **An asymmetric spinnaker provides a big power increase on this Omega. Mainsail, jib and spinnaker are sheeted in until they don't flap.**

The sheet is your accelerator

The sheets (ropes), which are used to pull in the sails, act like an accelerator. Pull the sheets in to power up the sails and drive the boat forwards; let the sheets out to depower the sails and slow the boat down.

Both mainsail and jib should be sheeted in at the correct angle to the wind. If a sail is not sheeted in far enough, it will flap and produce limited power. If a sail is sheeted in too far it will create turbulence, which reduces power. Either way, it does not allow the full power of the sail to drive you forward. So you've got to get the sheeting angle just right.

The perfect sheeting angle

Sails are not flat. Looking from the front (luff) to the back (leech), they have a curved shape (camber), which helps provide the power in the sail. What's more, the back edge (leech) of the sail also has a curve, which tends to lessen towards the top of the mast, producing a slightly twisted shape when seen from behind.

The result is that you cannot get a perfect sheeting angle for every part of the sail, but you can come close with a compromise. Telltales help you achieve this compromise. When the sail is correctly sheeted, telltales on both the windward and leeward side of the sail should stream back

Using telltales

Sail setting	Comment
CORRECT TRIM 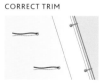	Telltales are parallel on both windward and leeward sides
UNDER TRIMMING 	The windward telltale is higher than it should be: pull in the sheet
OVER TRIMMING 	The leeward telltale is higher than it should be: let out the sheet

Above: **You can see the lowest telltales streaming perfectly on the jib.**

horizontally. When the windward telltales stream upwards you need to pull in the sheet. When the leeward telltales stream upwards you need to let out the sheet.

Taking off

If you sit in a dinghy and let all the sheets go, the boat will naturally lie side-on to the wind, which will blow slightly from ahead. In this position, the boat will be gently blown sideways by the wind, with the resistance of the daggerboard also driving it slightly ahead.

To take off, sit on the side of the boat, which should be balanced so it is virtually level, hold the tiller extension firmly in your back hand and move the rudder blade to its central 'straight ahead' position. Take the mainsheet in your front hand and pull it in slowly until the sail stops flapping. Keep sheeting in until the telltales are streaming horizontally on both sides. The boat will start sailing forwards.

Start sailing on a beam reach, with the wind blowing from the side. Experiment with pulling in the mainsail to speed up and letting it out to slow down.

Windward helm

Under sail power, many boats have a slight tendency to 'windward helm' or 'weather helm'. This means that if you let the tiller go, the boat will automatically turn up towards the wind. 'Windward helm' is indicated by a slight pull on the tiller extension. This is perfectly normal and has the added benefit of providing a more precise feel to steering the boat.

The opposite of windward helm is leeward helm, meaning that the boat has a natural tendency to sail away from the wind, which can make it difficult to control. Leeward helm is not desirable and should never be experienced if the boat has been correctly set up.

Keep it flat

All modern dinghies are designed to be sailed flat on the water with a minimal angle of heel. If you let the boat heel too far, it will start to slide sideways (making leeway) as the daggerboard fails to grip and windward helm will increase as the rudder blade lifts out of the water. If you cannot hold the boat upright, let out the sheet a little.

Left: **The crew of this boat demonstrate perfect trim – note how they hold the boat completely flat, with the stern just lifted out of the water.**

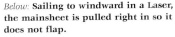

Below: **Sailing to windward in a Laser, the mainsheet is pulled right in so it does not flap.**

Rig controls

Sailing a dinghy requires more than just steering the boat. There are also rig controls, which are all operated by ropes. The primary control is the mainsheet, which adjusts the angle of the mainsail, while secondary controls such as the cunningham and kicking strap change its shape.

In addition to the coarse sheeting controls that adjust the angle of the sails to the wind, it's possible to tweak the shape of the sails to suit different conditions. For instance, sailing against the wind in a strong breeze calls for flat sails to reduce power and enable the boat to point close to the wind. However, on a reach in light airs a fuller, more curved sail will produce more drive.

Putting shape into sails

A mainsail or jib is not a simple triangle of cloth with three straight sides. To provide best performance, the sail must have an aerodynamic, curved shape, and to achieve this, a number of individual panels are joined together to create a sail with curved sides. This will then set in the correct shape and will respond to changes in halyard, clew outhaul and sheet tension. Generally, the

more tension that is applied to these controls, the flatter the sail will become and vice versa.

- ✪ The leech of a mainsail has a curved 'roach' (the area outside a straight line between tack and head) to increase the size and power of the sail. Battens are used to support this area.
- ✪ The foot of the mainsail has a slightly curved shape that helps wind flow across the bottom panel of the sail. Tensioning the foot of the sail by pulling on the clew outhaul will flatten the lower third of the sail.
- ✪ The luff is also cut with a curve, designed to match the way the mast bends when you go sailing.

Managing sail shape

As soon as you pull the mainsheet in, the mast will start to bend backwards and sideways. The

Above: **The mast of this Xenon bends in a curve that pulls the mainsail into a flatter shape. This helps to depower the sail in stronger winds.**

sophistication of the mast and rig controls will determine how much control you have over the way it bends and affects sail shape. An unstayed mast made from parallel-sided aluminium or glassfibre tube will provide minimal control; a fully stayed mast made from tapered aluminium or carbon fibre can

The dinghy rig

The arrangement of the mainsheet varies from dinghy to dinghy, although the principle remains the same. The mainsail is the largest sail and it can exert quite a strong pull on the mainsheet, which is normally managed by a system of blocks.

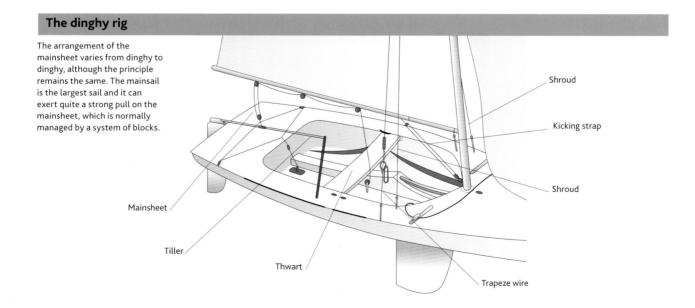

Shroud

Kicking strap

Shroud

Mainsheet

Tiller

Thwart

Trapeze wire

Left: **Too much power! For a quick solution, the helmsman should ease the mainsheet. For a more sophisticated and efficient solution, the crew should pull down the cunningham to flatten the sail and open the leech.**

Luff round

When you hoist the mainsail in the boat park, you have to pull the curved luff up a straight mast. This explains why the bolt rope may not slide up the mast as easily as you might expect.

Mainsheet and jib sheets

The sheets control the angle of each sail to the wind. Pulling the mainsheet in as hard as possible will also tighten the leech, which helps the boat point close to the wind in light or moderate breezes.

Cunningham

The cunningham is a downhaul control line attached to the luff of the mainsail, approximately 30cm (12in) above the boom. It is named after Briggs Swift Cunningham II, who skippered the 12-Metre *Columbia* to victory in the 1958 America's Cup. The cunningham allows the crew to adjust the amount

of luff tension in the mainsail while the boat is sailing, and is usually operated by control lines that lead to each side of the boat. Pulling down on the cunningham bends the mast, moving sail draft (curvature) forward and opening the leech, making it easier to handle the boat in stronger winds.

On a catamaran, the cunningham is replaced by a multi-purchase downhaul control, which is used to bend the mast and flatten the sail.

Below: **Perfect trim. Helm and crew are sailing this boat to windward beautifully. They have adjusted the sail shape as a perfect balance to their weight.**

provide a high degree of control, with spreaders, lower and upper shrouds, helping to dictate the degree and direction of bend.

What are rig controls for?

You do not want to go sailing with exactly the same power in light, moderate and strong winds. In light winds you need more power to drive the boat, but in stronger winds you need to reduce power to control the boat and keep it upright.

This is particularly important when sailing towards the wind, although when sailing downwind with the wind behind, full sail power can be used in most conditions.

Rig controls allow you to increase or decrease the amount of fullness (draft) in the mainsail, move the fullness forwards or backwards, and increase or decrease the way the mainsail twists from the bottom to the top of its leech.

Rig controls (2)

Controlling twist

The leech of a sail tends to twist from the bottom towards the top – if you look at a sail from behind, the bottom panel is normally twisted at a closer angle to the wind than the top panel.

Adjusting the amount of twist is useful for maintaining control of the boat. The top part of the mainsail can be transformed into a flat blade, which effectively creates no power and greatly reduces the heeling of the boat in stronger winds.

The amount of sail twist is governed by mainsheet and kicking strap tension. Tightening the mainsheet pulls the sail inwards at the bottom and downwards at the top. The downward pull of the kicking strap is used for more precise control over sail twist.

Kicking strap or boom vang

The kicking strap or boom vang is a control line between the mast and boom. Its original role was to hold the boom down at a horizontal angle, preventing it from riding

Above: **The gnav is an upside-down kicking strap that frees up the area below the boom directly behind the mast.**

Below: **The sail of this singlehander provides a beautiful foil for light winds with minimal cunningham and kicking strap tension.**

up when sailing downwind with the mainsheet eased. It plays an important role in regulating sail twist, bending the mast and tensioning the leech.

Dual control lines can be led to both sides of the boat for adjustment while sailing. On a catamaran, the boom is held down by mainsheet tension at the back of the boat so a kicking strap is not required.

Some boats are fitted with a gnav – vang spelt backwards – which performs exactly the same function but uses an aluminium strut above the boom, leaving more space for the crew. The angle of the gnav is adjusted by sliding it along a track mounted on the top of the boom.

In light winds up to force 2:

- No cunningham and kicking strap tension is needed
- Outhaul can be tensioned to promote better airflow over the flattened lower part of the sail.

Outhaul

The outhaul control line is led from the clew of the mainsail along the boom. If it is tightened, the outhaul will flatten the lower section of the mainsail and move the area of maximum draft further aft.

TIP

On a catamaran, sail twist can be controlled by using mainsheet tension at different positions on the full-length traveller across the rear beam. This allows the mainsail to be sheeted hard in at any angle to the apparent wind.

Right: **The slot between jib and mainsail accelerates wind flow. A wider slot makes the rig easier to control as the wind increases.**

When to use sail controls

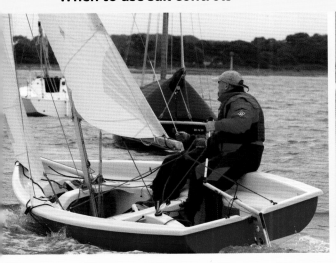

In moderate winds below force 3:

✪ Moderate amount of kicking strap tension can be used to promote mainsail leech twist, reducing power in the top of the sail, making the boat easier to hold upright
✪ No cunningham tension is required
✪ The outhaul can be eased to provide maximum power at the bottom of the mainsail.

In strong winds over force 4:

✪ The object is to completely depower the top of the mainsail for sailing towards the wind
✪ Maximum kicker, cunningham and outhaul tension are used to bend the mast. This stretches and flattens the sail, moving all power forwards. The top half of the sail twists open and becomes a flat, powerless blade aligned with the wind.

Sail power and apparent wind

Sails need to be set at the optimum angle to the wind to provide smooth airflow over both sides of the sail. An underwater foil such as a centreboard or daggerboard stops the boat from being blown sideways.

Pressure drives the sails

Unless you are sailing directly downwind, modern rigs are designed so that wind flows over both sides of the sails. The wind separates when it hits the leading edge of each sail and accelerates round its two curved sides. This creates high pressure on the windward side of the sail and low pressure on the leeward side. The difference between these pressures creates a force that sucks the sail to leeward, pushing the boat forwards.

Forwards not sideways

Unless the wind is blowing directly from behind, there's always a component of the force on the sail that tends to push the boat sideways. This is strongest when a boat is sailing at a slow speed towards the wind. The centreboard or daggerboard provides natural resistance to the boat being pushed sideways and also generates a lifting force. It's most efficient when

pointing straight downwards – one reason it's important to keep the boat upright, rather than allowing it to heel.

Sheeting the sails

The crew set the angle of each sail relative to the boat and the wind by adjusting a rope called a sheet, pulling it in or letting it out as necessary. On a boat with two sails, adjusting the width of the slot – the narrow passage between the headsail and mainsail – plays an important role in how effectively air flows over the leeward side of the mainsail.

Telltales can be fitted to the sail to indicate when there's smooth airflow over both sides of the sail (see p44).

True and apparent wind

True wind is the wind direction and speed encountered when you stand still, or when your boat is stationary. However, as soon as you start moving, this very movement

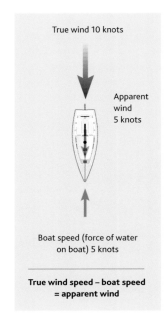

Above: **A boat's motion modifies the wind that is experienced, creating the apparent wind in which the boat sails.**

modifies the speed and direction of the wind that you experience.

If the true wind speed is 10 knots and you were to head directly into the wind at 5 knots, the apparent wind speed would be 15 knots. Conversely, if you were to sail directly away from a 10-knot breeze at a speed of 5 knots, the apparent

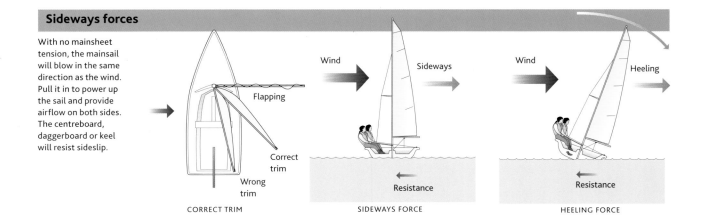

Sideways forces

With no mainsheet tension, the mainsail will blow in the same direction as the wind. Pull it in to power up the sail and provide airflow on both sides. The centreboard, daggerboard or keel will resist sideslip.

CORRECT TRIM

SIDEWAYS FORCE

HEELING FORCE

wind would then be only 5 knots. Apparent wind is always strongest when beating towards the wind and weakest when running downwind.

Apparent wind direction

True and apparent wind will only blow from exactly the same direction when the boat is sailing directly downwind. Sailing in any other direction, the wind induced by the forward motion of the boat changes the angle of the apparent wind.

The faster you travel, the greater the difference between the direction of the true wind and the apparent wind, with the latter always from further ahead than the true wind.

This explains why spectacularly fast sailing craft will have sails pulled in at a tight angle to the wind, even when sailing on a broad-reaching course with the true wind direction behind the boat.

Above: **A dinghy such as this Xenon is designed to be sailed flat, not heeled, for maximum efficiency.**

Below: **Sailing with the wind directly behind, apparent wind is reduced. This Enterprise is goosewinging with the jib held out to windward.**

Rig and hull balance

While the rudder is the primary means of steering a dinghy, a number of other factors have a significant influence, including sail trim and the position of the crew's weight.

The balance of a boat's rig depends on the relationship between the centre of effort of the rig and the centre of lateral resistance of the underwater appendages – the rudder and daggerboard or centreboard.

Designers aim to position these so that the boat will have a slight tendency to turn up towards the wind. This gives a more positive feel to the helm and is also a useful safety feature – if you accidentally let go of the tiller the boat should turn up towards the wind, instead of bearing away into a crash gybe.

Effect of sails on steering

The mainsail is behind the centre of lateral resistance, so power in this sail tends to make the boat turn up towards the wind. By contrast, the jib is forward of the centre of lateral resistance, so power in the jib tends to make the boat turn away from the wind. With perfectly balanced sails the boat will move ahead with a balanced helm.

Easing the mainsheet (thereby depowering the sail) will allow the power in the jib to turn the bow away from the wind. Sheeting the mainsail back in (thereby increasing the power in the sail) will make the boat luff back up towards the wind.

Effect of heel

When a boat heels, due to the power of the wind in the sails, it will tend to turn up towards the wind for two reasons – firstly, the immersed part of the hull changes from a symmetrical shape to a skewed form that tends to turn the boat towards the wind. Secondly, the rig is no

Below: **A dinghy is always at its most efficient when it's kept flat – even in strong winds!**

Perfect balance

With perfectly balanced sails the boat will move ahead with balanced helm. If there is too much drive from the mainsail the boat will turn towards the wind. This is known as weather helm. If there is too much drive from the jib, the boat will turn away from the wind. This is known as lee helm.

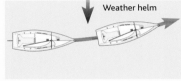

Balanced helm

SAILS SET CORRECTLY

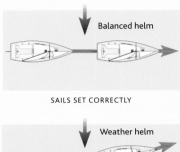

Weather helm

MAINSAIL TOO TIGHT

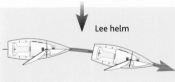

Lee helm

MAINSAIL OUT TOO FAR

Above: **If necessary hike (lean out) hard and depower the sails to keep the boat as flat as possible.**

Below: **Balancing the boat and its sails is important for steering a high-performance dinghy such as the National 12.**

longer directly above the centre of lateral resistance – it's now out over the side of the boat. This in turn means the power of the sails exerts a turning moment that tends to turn the boat towards the direction of the wind.

Sailing without a rudder

We can harness these effects to make it possible to sail the boat without a rudder. This is generally easiest when sailing towards the wind, as the wind flow over the sails makes this a dynamically stable point of sailing.

In moderate conditions, often all that's needed is to ease the mainsheet by a few inches – this will reduce the extent to which the sail is turning the boat towards the wind, and she will steer a straight course.

You can also use crew weight to steer the boat – moving weight to starboard will make the boat tend to turn to port and vice versa – and this is important if sailing on a reach or run without a rudder.

Practising sailing without a rudder helps experienced sailors to sharpen their skills and can be especially useful for those who race competitively – every time you move the rudder there is a little extra drag over it, which slows the boat. Therefore, the more that you use your weight to help steer, the faster you will sail.

Rigging & launching

Rigging a simple dinghy

A small dinghy such as a Topper, Pico or Laser has the simplest possible rig that is very quick to assemble. Rigging for all these dinghies follows the same procedure, with slight variations.

Rigging a simple dinghy

Unpack the components
- Sleeved two-part mast made of aluminium or glassfibre tube.
- Boom made of aluminium tube.
- Sail made of Dacron with an optional set of plastic battens.
- Daggerboard, rudder, tiller and tiller extension.
- Rope set including downhaul and outhaul lines for the mainsail, kicking strap, traveller line and mainsheet with blocks.

Assemble the mast and sail
- Place the boat on the beach or on its trolley, angled so that the bow is pointing directly into the wind.
- Push the two halves of the mast together. Avoid getting sand or grit in the joint, as this may make it difficult to pull the mast apart.
- Unfold the sail and lay it out on the ground. Align the luff tube or sock along the edge of the sail with the wind direction, with the bottom corner (tack) closest to the wind and the top corner (head) furthest from the wind.
- The sail on a dinghy like the Laser needs three stiff battens to support the roach. Push each batten into its pocket in the leech, ensuring the outer end is locked into the sail.
- Pull the luff tube down over the mast. Note that unlike most other luff-tube dinghies, the Topper also has a main halyard, which attaches to the top of the sail and passes down through the luff tube.

Put the mast in the boat
- Roll the sail so that it is tightly wrapped around the mast.
- Lift the mast vertically, then lower its mast base into the deck socket. Both the Pico and the Topper have a locking system to hold the mast in place.

Complete the rigging
- Attach the boom to the mast, just below the tack of the sail. The Pico and the Topper both have a plastic jaw that fits over the mast. The Laser has a more conventional gooseneck pin that fits into the mast.
- Attach the traveller line to the stern of the boat.
- Attach one end of the mainsheet to the boom. Pull the mainsheet through the blocks on the boom, traveller line and cockpit floor. Use a figure-of-eight knot to secure the free end of the mainsheet.
- With the boat pointing into the wind, unfurl the sail and attach the outhaul line to the clew. This will hold the boom horizontally beneath the foot of the sail.
- Pull down and tension the downhaul (also known as a cunningham) line, which is attached to the tack of the sail.

Below (left to right): **1. Sort out all the components before you start rigging the boat. 2. Most mainsails need battens. 3. Make sure the battens are securely** locked into their pockets. **4. Pull the luff tube of the sail down over the mast. 5. Lift the mast vertically. If it's windy you may need an extra pair of hands** to keep it steady. **6. Drop the mast into its deck socket. 7. The mainsheet is connected to the traveller line at the transom.**

○ Attach the kicking strap between the mast and boom.

Ready to go

○ Lay the daggerboard in the cockpit, ensuring it is attached to the shock-cord retainer, to prevent it from falling out of the boat.

○ Drop the rudder onto the stainless steel pintles (pins) on the stern of the boat. The rudder must lock on to the pintles so that it can't fall off in a capsize.

○ Insert the tiller into the rudder head, ensuring it is free to move from side to side beneath the mainsheet traveller line. Attach the tiller extension.

○ Make sure the drainage bung and any drainage hatches are secure.

○ Tension the outhaul, downhaul and kicking strap wrinkles from the sail.

TIP

Beware of the mainsail taking control when you lift the mast. If the sail has no battens, you can wrap it tightly around the mast to prevent it blowing like a flag.

Below: **Attach and tension the downhaul, outhaul and kicking strap, which will help control the shape of the mainsail.**

Rigging a twin-crew dinghy

Most dinghies specifically designed to be sailed by two crew have a more complex rig supported by wire shrouds and a forestay. Rigging is similar for all twin-crew boats, but there are many variations in the process for different designs.

Rigging a twin-crew dinghy

Putting up the mast

On most boats the mast of a twin-crew dinghy can be left up for the whole season. It only needs to be lowered if the dinghy is being road trailed or put in winter storage.

Putting up the mast normally requires two people. Depending on the boat, the mast may range from very light (especially if it is carbon) to quite heavy. Make sure that shrouds, forestay and any trapeze wires are untangled.

✪ Lift up the mast and place its base on the mast step, which may be located at deck or cockpit floor level. Some dinghies have a mast gate, which will lock the mast in position while the shrouds and forestay are attached.

✪ If there is no mast gate, one person must hold the mast steady while the other attaches the two shrouds to adjustable fittings (chain plates) on the sides of the boat.

✪ Attach the wire forestay to the chain plate. Some dinghies have a conventional wire forestay, which attaches to a chain plate on the bow. Others rely on a wire inside the luff of the jib as the forestay, which holds up the mast, so a length of rope can act as a temporary forestay before the jib is attached.

✪ Many dinghies have a roller-furling jib. The tack (bottom corner) of the jib is attached by a shackle to the roller on the bow.

✪ The head of the sail is attached to a furling swivel on the end of the jib halyard, which is pulled up the mast. The jib can be furled when not in use.

✪ Pull down hard on the halyard, either using a multi-purchase block or lever system. This produces rigid tension on the jib luff and prevents it being blown into a curved shape.

Rigging the mainsail

Make sure the boat is secure on its trolley with the bow pointing directly into the wind.

✪ Place the rolled mainsail in the cockpit so that the luff (identified by its thick 'bolt rope' edge) is next to the mast.

✪ Unroll the mainsail and insert the battens. Lock them securely.

✪ Attach the main halyard to the head of the sail. Pull on the halyard and feed the bolt rope into the slot on the mast (mast track).

✪ One person should pull the halyard while the other feeds the bolt rope into the slot, ensuring it doesn't jam.

✪ Pull the mainsail to the top of the mast and secure the halyard.

Rigging the boom

✪ The boom is attached to the mast by a 'gooseneck' fitting. It will be held in a horizontal position when the mainsail is raised. The

Below (left to right): **1. Step the mast and attach the shrouds and forestay. 2. The RS500 shown here has an adjustable forestay. 3. Attach the luff of the jib to the forestay. 4. Attach the halyard to the head of the jib. 5. Pull up the jib halyard until it is taut. 6. Unroll the mainsail. 7. Attach the halyard, feed the bolt rope into the mast track and start pulling up the halyard. 8. As it goes up, make sure the bolt rope feeds into the mast track. Lock the halyard when the sail can go no higher.**

angle of the boom is controlled by a kicking strap that pulls down or a gnav (inverted 'vang'), which pushes down against the sail.

✿ A centre mainsheet connects twin blocks on the boom to a jamming block in the cockpit floor where it is led through a jamming cleat. This allows the helm to leave the mainsheet in a locked position.

Attaching the foils

✿ The rudder slides down on pintles mounted on the transom and should be locked in position.

✿ The tiller is inserted into the rudder head, where a pin may be used to lock it in position. The tiller extension can be attached with a twist-grip fitting.

✿ The daggerboard should be laid in the cockpit, ready for use by the crew. If the boat is fitted with a centreboard, then it must be fully retracted.

Final rigging

✿ Attach jib sheets to the clew of the jib and lead them through blocks or fairleads on either side of the boat.

✿ Tension the downhaul and outhaul lines to remove creases for the mainsail. Apply sufficient kicking strap tension to prevent the boom lifting.

Right: **The downhaul is used to tension the luff of the mainsail and can be adjusted while sailing.**

TIP

Take your time and make sure all the rigging is done correctly. You don't want anything to fail when you're out on the water! The bow must be facing into the wind when you rig the boat.

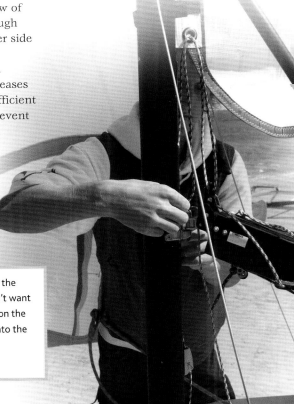

Rigging a catamaran

The 'platform' of a catamaran, formed by the hulls, beams and trampoline, is normally left fully assembled. Raising or lowering the mast for trailing or storage is straightforward, but requires two people to pull and push it upright due to the extra weight of its elliptical-shaped spar.

Raising the mast

Make sure the catamaran is level, either resting on its trailer or on the ground. Two people will be needed to raise the mast – due to the elliptical wing shape on a cat, it tends to be considerably heavier than on a dinghy. Make sure that shrouds, forestay and trapeze wires are not tangled.

- ✪ Lay the mast across the two beams with the mast base pointing forwards.
- ✪ Attach the two shrouds to shroud plates on each hull.
- ✪ Remove the security pin from the mast base, which is then locked on to the mast step ball in the middle of the forward beam.
- ✪ With the mast base secure, one person can walk the mast upright, lifting it hand over hand, while the other guides it and keeps it steady by pulling on the forestay.

✪ When the mast is upright, the forestay is attached to the chain plate or roller-furler on the wire bridle, which is connected to the bows of both hulls.

Tensioning the rig

Most cats have one or two trapeze wires on both sides of the boat. Each wire has a trapeze ring on the end. A shock-cord and line connects the trapeze ring to the boat, ensuring the trapeze wire stays taut when not being used. Cats perform best with the mast raked back at an angle of about ten degrees; trapeze wires can be used to tension the rig on land.

- ✪ One person pulls back on the trapeze wire on one side, while the other person tightens the shroud.
- ✪ Repeat on the other side.

Attaching rudders and tillers

Cats have a separate rudder on each hull. It is quite time-consuming to attach or detach rudders, so they are generally left on for the season. The tillers on each rudder are connected by a longitudinal tiller bar, which slots down over a pin at each end.

- ✪ Fix the rudders with conventional dinghy pintles, or secure by a full-length stainless steel pin designed to cope with heavier loads.
- ✪ The tiller bar has an adjustable-length mechanism to ensure that both rudder blades are parallel. You can normally judge this by eye, or measure the distance between the leading and trailing edges of each blade.
- ✪ Make sure the pin that attaches the tiller extension to the tiller bar is secured in place.

Rigging a catamaran

Hoisting the mainsail

A cat's mainsail has full-length battens to maintain the shape of the sail under heavy load.

Below: A fully powered-up cat has heavy loads on its rig and rudders. Make sure everything is perfect before you set sail.

- Unroll the sail and tension each batten to remove wrinkles before hoisting the sail.
- Attach the main halyard and feed the head and bolt rope into the mast track. One person will need to feed the bolt rope into the track while the other pulls on the halyard. Due to full-length battens in the sail, it may feel quite heavy and hard to pull to the top of the mast.
- Most cats have a system that locks the head of the sail to the top of the mast. Pull the sail up as far as it will go, and then pull it down by a centimetre or so until it locks, either with a stainless steel ring (which drops over a peg) or a ferrule (which jams against a pair of jaws). Luff tension is vital for best performance on a cat and is provided by a multi-purchase downhaul.

Attaching the mainsheet

- Attach the multi-purchase mainsheet to the rear beam and lead it through the traveller control. This then allows a continuous control line to be used for both the mainsheet and the traveller adjustment.

Below (left to right): **1.** Lift the mast with shrouds attached. **2.** Use the trapezes to tension the shrouds. **3.** Unroll the sail and attach the halyard. **4.** One crew pulls the sail up while the other guides it into the mast track. **5.** Make sure the mainsheet is untangled. **6.** Always check the bungs. **7.** A pin holds the tiller extension on to the tiller bar – make sure it is secure.

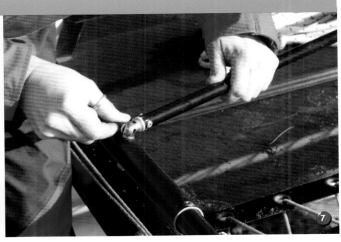

Launching a dinghy

There are a number of factors to consider when launching. Which is the best direction for the wind to be blowing? Do you need to think about tides? What surface is best to launch your boat from? Are there any dangers to avoid?

Offshore wind

With the wind blowing away from the shore it should be easy to leave, but you will get a false impression of the conditions. The water will appear to be flat close to the shore and the wind may be light and gusty as it blows past buildings, trees and other obstacles. However, the wind will get stronger the further from the shore you sail. This can be a real danger if you capsize or struggle to control the boat. You will be blown out into stronger winds and rougher water, making it more difficult to get back to shore safely.

Onshore wind

With the wind blowing on to the shore, you will have a clear idea of the conditions at sea. However, leaving the shore will be more difficult, especially if waves are breaking on the beach. In these conditions, as you beat away from the shore each wave tends to drive the boat back. Landing may also be difficult, particularly in big waves.

Cross-shore wind

This is perfect for launching or landing. The wind is blowing from the side, so you can sail out on a beam reach, then tack or gybe and sail back on a beam reach, turning the boat head-to-wind to stop when you reach shallow water.

Right: **The wind here is onshore. The crew will push the bow away before getting in, ensuring their boat avoids the moored dinghies in front.**

Left: **Cross-shore wind, blowing parallel to the shore, is perfect for launching and landing. But deep water could make it difficult to hold on to this Hobie 16.**

Tidal effects

There may be a big difference between launching and landing at different states of the tide. At low water, there may be a lot of sand or mud to pull your boat across. At other states of tide, the sea may reach a steeply shelving part of the beach where it is impossible to hold the boat while standing in the water.

TIP

Be courteous to other people on the beach, swimming or in the launch area. They may not understand if you are struggling with the boat.

Always be aware of the direction in which the tide is flowing and the time at which it will change. If the tide flows in the same direction as the wind, the sea will be relatively smooth. If the tide flows against the wind, the sea will be heaped up into short, uncomfortable waves. If sailing in an estuary or near a significant headland, be aware of tidal streams that will sweep you out to sea – it's safer to sail with an incoming tide.

Pulling a dinghy overland

Pulling a light boat across hard sand is easy; pulling a heavy boat across soft sand may be impossible. If the trolley wheels start to sink, get someone to help. Shingle is very difficult to pull a dinghy over and the boat must be firmly secured to its trolley. Rubber mats or tracks are laid down by sailing clubs to overcome this problem. Concrete is perfect, but becomes slippery if seaweed is not cleared away. Wear sailing boots or shoes for grip and beware of falling under the boat.

Left: **When the tide goes out, there may be a lot of mud. Time your sailing accordingly! Despite the low tide, these sailors have sufficiently solid ground to push their boats down to the water on trolleys.**

Obstructions and dangers

When launching a dinghy beware of the following:

- ❂ Keep clear of swimmers when launching or landing your boat.
- ❂ Watch out for moored boats.
- ❂ Look out for small powercraft: a jet ski driver may be going too fast with little comprehension of the 'rules of the road'.
- ❂ Check for underwater obstructions (such as a rock or reef) that may be covered by the tide. Consult a chart or ask a local sailor with experience.

Right: **Places to land and launch can get busy. Never barge in; offer to help with other people's trolleys.**

Launching methods

Are you ready to sail? Launching a dinghy with two crew has the advantage that one can hold the boat while the other pulls the trolley back to the shore. If you are launching singlehanded, seek help from a volunteer who doesn't mind getting wet feet!

Ready to sail

Experienced crews will often rig the dinghy before launching, keeping the bow pointing into the wind to stop it blowing over. However, novice crews may find it easier to hoist the sails once the boat is afloat.

If you are pulling the boat down the slipway or beach with the mainsail already hoisted, beware of the dinghy blowing over – the bow must be kept towards the wind, with the crew ready to hold down the boat's windward side if necessary. The mainsheet must also be uncleated so that it can run free.

Before launching, make sure the boat is correctly rigged, with everything secure and stowed. Don't forget the drainage bung or plug, which is usually in the transom of the boat. This must be screwed in tight. Make sure the rudder blade is locked in the fully lifted position. If possible, always fit the rudder before launch. It can be very difficult to engage the pintles when the boat is swinging around on the water.

Launching with two crew

When launching with two crew:
- ❂ Use the trolley to pull the dinghy into deep enough water where it will slide off and float – normally about knee height for the crew.
- ❂ One crew should take the trolley ashore. Leave it in a safe place above the high water mark, without creating an obstruction for people on the shore.
- ❂ The other crew must hold the boat. If it's a stable design, you can hold it by the bow and let it blow downwind. If it is unstable, like a skiff, you may need to hold it by the windward shroud, keeping it pointing at a slight angle towards the wind.
- ❂ The crew should be first to get on board, either over the windward side or over the transom of an open cockpit boat. If necessary, the crew can now hoist the sails.
- ❂ Standing or sitting in the middle of the boat, the crew should partly lower the centreboard or daggerboard to give some control and prevent the boat going sideways once the sails are sheeted in.

Using the launching trolley

Launch the dinghy on a shore or slipway with a launching trolley. When in the water get your crew to hold the boat by the bow and into wind, while you climb in and hoist the sails.

Launch into the water.

You can also launch the dinghy stern-first, whereby the dinghy will swing off with her stern downwind. Launching stern-first can also ease the removal of the trolley, and is safer with a heavy boat and steep slipway.

Wind direction

Remove the launching trolley and return it to the trolley park.

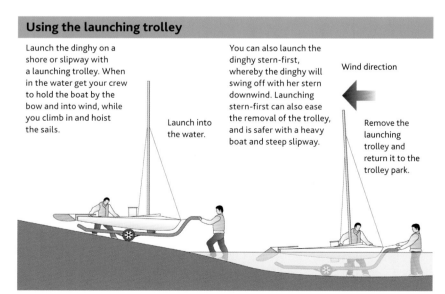

Above: **With the wind blowing on to the shore, this crew pulls their boat bows-first into the water until it is deep enough to slide off the trolley.**

Above: **The crew of this RS800 inserts the tip of the daggerboard in its case, while the helm steadies the boat by holding the windward rack.**

- Depending on the depth of water, the crew should also partly lower the rudder blade.
- With a cross-shore wind, when the crew is ready, the helm turns the boat on to a beam reach, then grabs the tiller extension to control the rudder, and gets in over the windward side. At the same time, the crew balances the boat and unfurls the jib, sheeting in to help the boat bear away from the wind and gather speed.
- As soon as the water is deep enough, the helm must lower the rudder blade and lock it in the fully down position. It is not possible to steer the boat properly with the rudder blade partially lifted, as this will create very heavy weather helm (see Tip). The crew must also lower the centreboard or daggerboard to the optimum position for the initial point of sail (see p43).

Launching singlehanded

If you are alone, get someone to help retrieve the trolley while you hold the boat.

- Pull the boat into thigh-deep water, holding the bow into the wind. When you are ready to go, grab the side of the boat just behind the mast and push the daggerboard halfway down. Then move quickly to the back of the boat and push the rudder halfway down.
- With a cross-shore wind, push the bow away from the wind so that the boat is on a beam reach.
- Step up into the cockpit, while pushing away with your back foot.
- Sheet in the mainsail to move away from the shore. As soon as the water is deep enough, let go of the mainsheet to slow the boat so that you can push both the daggerboard and the rudder all the way down.

TIP

As soon as the water is deep enough, make sure the rudder is locked right down. If it is not in the fully down position, you will feel weather helm on the tiller (pulling away) when you sheet in the sail.

Above: **When you leave the shore, it's vital to get the rudder fully down as soon as possible. Check everything is working.**

Sailing away from the shore

If the wind is blowing cross-shore, you should have no problems sailing away on a beam reach. However, if the wind is blowing offshore or onshore, different techniques are needed for a smooth getaway.

Launching in an offshore wind

With the wind blowing the boat into deeper water this is relatively easy – but you must ensure there's enough room to turn the boat around as you leave the shore. Start by identifying whether turning to port or starboard will get you away from the shore the quickest.

- Hoist the mainsail onshore, with the sheet slack. With the boat head-to-wind push it stern-first into the water, ensuring that the rudder blade is locked fully upright.

- Push the trolley into deep enough water to slide the boat off. Get the crew to hold the bow, while the helm gets on board and lowers the rudder to the fully down position: this should be possible as the stern is in deeper water.

- The centreboard or daggerboard should be partly lowered to ensure the boat will respond to the helm. With the board fully raised the boat will just slide sideways and won't answer readily to movements of the rudder.

- When you are ready to go, the crew pushes the bow as far as possible away from the wind, jumping on board once the boat begins to accelerate. To help the bow bear away quickly, the helm should unfurl the jib and 'back' it by pulling in the windward sheet. The wind blowing against the wrong side of the jib will push the bow away from the shore quickly.

- As soon as the boat is facing away from the shore, let go of the windward jib sheet, straighten out your course and sheet the sail in on the new side.

Below: **Make sure everything is ready before you start sailing. Check to see how much space you need to avoid other boats.**

Launching in an onshore wind

It can be tricky to sail away from the shore in an onshore wind, when waves may push your boat back onto the beach.

Check the angle of the boat with the bow pointing directly into the wind. If the starboard side of the boat is nearest to the beach, sail away on a starboard tack and vice versa.

- It may be possible to launch the fully rigged boat by pulling the trolley bows-first into the water, if the water isn't too deep.

- Alternatively, you can launch the dinghy stern-first in an onshore wind with the mainsail lowered and jib furled. The crew should push the boat out to the deepest possible water, hold the bows while the helm climbs on board to hoist the mainsail, then jump on board when the boat is ready to sail.

Left: **Wait your turn to leave in an onshore wind, when speed and power are needed to get away.**

Launching a catamaran

When launching in an offshore wind, it can be difficult to turn the boat without sailing back onto the shore. One way to overcome this is to reverse away from the shore.

✪ Catamarans have a launch trolley with a single axle and two large wheels. Push the trolley under the hulls so that it is at the balance point close to the shrouds.

✪ Launch the cat stern-first. Then sit on each bow, to lift the sterns and let the cat slowly sail backwards away from the shore. The crew can then climb onto the trampoline and make the turn.

Above: **Cat sailors have a novel way of leaving the shore in an offshore wind – simply sail out backwards, with both crew sitting on the bows!**

✪ Before attempting to sail away, lower the rudder and centreboard or daggerboard as far as possible: ideally the rudder should be fully down. If possible, choose a moment to leave with a favourable wind shift – this will help you get away from the shore faster.

✪ Keep plenty of power and speed up to sail through the waves. Turn the bow slightly towards each wave, and then bear away to accelerate as soon as the wave has passed. This will make your passage more comfortable and less bumpy.

TIP

A singlehanded dinghy won't have a jib to help it turn. Push the bow offwind until it is pointing away from the shore; allow a wide arc to leeward to guarantee completing the turn.

Getting off the shore

Getting away in an offshore wind: Give a shove off and move into water deep enough to put the centreboard or daggerboard and the rudder fully down.

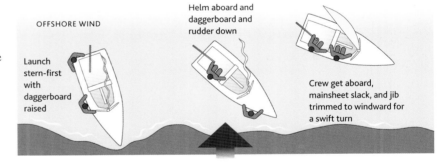

OFFSHORE WIND

Launch stern-first with daggerboard raised

Helm aboard and daggerboard and rudder down

Crew get aboard, mainsheet slack, and jib trimmed to windward for a swift turn

Getting away in an onshore wind: With the wind blowing towards the shore you need to move away from the launch site. When you can manoeuvre, turn the boat and pick up the wind in the sails.

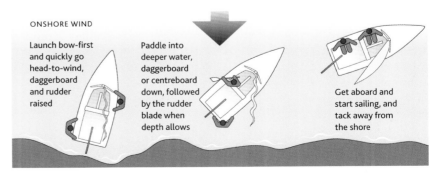

ONSHORE WIND

Launch bow-first and quickly go head-to-wind, daggerboard and rudder raised

Paddle into deeper water, daggerboard or centreboard down, followed by the rudder blade when depth allows

Get aboard and start sailing, and tack away from the shore

Coming back to shore

At the end of a great sailing session it is time to sail back, land on the shore and pull your boat out of the water. It is important to plan ahead before you make your final approach. The tide or the wind may have changed and there may be more people on the shore.

Returning to shore

Has anything changed?
Tides: If you are sailing in a tidal area, the water could be a lot higher or lower than when you launched. If the water is higher, the angle of the beach may have changed from gently shelving to a steeply shelving shore. When you jump out of the boat, the water may be a lot deeper than you expect. If the water is lower, rocks and other underwater obstructions may be dangerously close to the surface. When you land, the trolley may be a long way up the beach, which is tricky if you are sailing singlehanded. It may also be a long way to pull the trolley across soft sand or mud.

Wind: Has the wind changed direction since you launched? An offshore wind in the morning may have changed to an onshore sea breeze in the afternoon. Flat water has now become waves breaking on the shore, which could make it tricky to land.

People and boats: Did you launch early in the day? If you return on a fine summer's afternoon you can expect to have to manoeuvre past swimmers by the shore, sunbathers on the beach or other dinghies jostling for position on the slipway.

Approaching in a cross-shore wind
As with launching and sailing off the beach, landing should be straightforward in a cross-shore wind.
- Sail in towards the beach on a beam reach. Look ahead to make sure your landing spot is clear. If the slipway is blocked by other boats or there are children swimming in the water, change your landing site or wait for the jam to clear.
- If you have a furling jib, roll it away to slow the boat down. When sailing on a beam reach, remember that you can only slow right down by luffing (pushing the tiller away) towards the wind.
- Leave the rudder right down until

you are ready to stop the boat and get over the side. You should aim to sail into water that is little more than thigh deep. If you partially lift the rudder, the boat will develop strong weather helm and become difficult to steer.
- The daggerboard or centreboard will require more depth than the rudder, but leave them down for as long as possible for best control. You can still steer the boat with the board partially retracted.
- As the boat enters shallow water, slow down by gently luffing into the wind.
- Stop before the rudder blade touches the bottom! Turn the boat directly into the wind so that it will come to a dead halt.
- The crew should jump over the side and grab the windward shroud or forestay to hold the boat steady. The helm must raise the rudder and lock it, before pulling up the centreboard or pulling out the daggerboard.

Below (left to right): **1. Approach the shore and slow down with the daggerboard or centreboard partially retracted. 2. Turn into the wind to stop, and let the crew hop over the side. 3. Grab the bow and** hold the boat so it is facing into the wind. **4. Push the trolley under the boat so it is fully supported and level. 5. You may have to lash the trolley handle to the bow.**

- The helm should retrieve the trolley. Walk it into water that is deep enough to pull the dinghy onto its supports. When you do this, the trolley must be aligned with the wind.
- Depending on wind strength, it may be necessary to drop the mainsail before you pull the boat and trolley up the beach. If the mainsail is hoisted, the bow must be kept pointing into the wind when you drop the sails.

TIP

If the mainsail is hoisted, let off the cunningham and kicking strap controls to reduce power in the sail. Make sure the mainsheet can run free.

Above: **How are you going to get ashore? A small dinghy such as the Taz can be carried up the beach by a couple of willing adults or put on a trolley.**

Coming back to shore (2)

Approaching in an offshore wind

The wind will be blowing off the shore, with flat water likely to make the approach straightforward. But the wind will not let you sail straight to the shore. You will need to sail a zigzag tacking course towards the shore, pointing the boat a little way from your destination on your final approach. This means you can sail in on a close reach, with the option of heading up or bearing away.

⊘ Be aware of leeway on the final approach. If the beach is gently shelving, the daggerboard or centreboard may need to be partly lifted when the boat is still some way out.

⊘ When you are close to the shore and don't need to point high, furl the jib to slow down. To lose more speed, ease the mainsheet until the mainsail starts flapping.

⊘ Fully retract the centreboard or pull out the daggerboard before the rudder touches the bottom. The crew should immediately jump out on the windward side and hold the boat by the shroud or forestay.

Approaching in an onshore wind

When the wind is blowing onshore, waves may make the approach difficult and there could be problems stopping the boat. The solution is to reduce speed to a minimum.

⊘ In light winds, you may be able to sail into shallow water and turn the boat through 180 degrees so that it stops with the bow pointing into the wind. Be aware that the water could be a lot deeper at the bow than the stern, making it difficult for the crew to hold the boat, particularly if there are waves.

⊘ Sailing towards the beach in stronger winds, you can furl the jib to slow down but you can't let out the mainsail. Luffing side-

TIP

If you are sailing in clear water, it is easy to assess the depth and know when it's time to stop the boat. In murky water and some lakes, it is impossible to see the bottom. You will have to check people standing in the water, or simply guess the depth.

Below: **If you try to catch the bow of a boat, make sure it is moving slowly. Don't get trapped in deep water with big waves between the bow and the shore.**

on to the wind will depower the mainsail but also turns the boat side-on to the waves, making it unstable. And your boat will be heading in the wrong direction!

- The seamanlike solution is to drop the mainsail before making the final approach (only possible on a double-handed dinghy with a conventional main halyard).
- Turn the boat head-to-wind in flat water, before you get into waves, which will build up closer to the shore. Drop the mainsail quickly and stow it in the cockpit.
- Lift the centreboard or daggerboard, and then back the jib to help turn the boat and sail in towards the beach. On the final approach, furl the jib or let the sheet go so that you slow right down.
- The crew can jump out on the windward side, grab the side of the boat and let it turn into the wind while the helm raises the rudder.

TIP

You want to stop the boat exactly when the water is not too shallow or too deep. If it's too shallow, you may damage the rudder or board. If it's too deep, you may be too buoyant for your feet to grip the seabed.

Below: **Approaching the beach in an onshore wind is not a problem in light winds. But in strong winds it may be necessary to drop the mainsail and stow it in the cockpit, before making a final approach at slow speed. Note that this Merlin Rocket has no rudder! The helm has removed the fixed rudder for the final approach, and is just steering with the sails.**

Coming back to shore (3)

Landing singlehanded

With no crew to help pull up the daggerboard or hold the boat, you have to plan ahead before making the final approach.

- When the wind is cross-shore or offshore, ease the mainsheet to slow the boat down, while keeping enough speed to steer.
- Most singlehanded dinghies have a daggerboard. Pull it halfway up on the final approach, then let off the rudder downhaul, attached to the side of the tiller.
- As you sail into shallow water, lift the daggerboard higher to make sure it can't hit the ground.
- Turn the boat into the wind and get out over the windward side. Pull out the daggerboard and lay it in the cockpit. Pull up the rudder blade fully.
- In light winds, you may be able to leave the boat in shallow water and run ashore to get the trolley. In strong winds, you'll need help.

Sailing in on waves

If the wind is blowing onshore, you will need to luff on to a beam reach to depower the sail and slow down, jump out, and spin the boat so that it is facing into the wind. When it is very windy and there are waves, sail in with the daggerboard lifted and rudder blade released, keeping your weight well back in the boat to avoid pushing the bow into a wave. Look for a flat spot between the waves to luff, jump out and grab the boat. If there are breaking waves, it may be impossible to use a trolley. The boat needs to be carried quickly to shore.

Landing a catamaran

- Furl the jib to reduce power on the final approach.

Landing a catamaran

Above (left to right): **1. Waiting to be pulled back up the beach; the crew has gone to fetch the Cat Trax set of wheels.**

Above: **Is anyone going to help you when you reach the shore? It's handy, even in a light wind.**

Above right: **Most singlehanders are light enough for one person to pull up the slipway. The Phantom is made of superlight epoxy sandwich construction.**

- It is very difficult to steer a cat if the rudders are not right down, so leave them down until you stop and the crew have jumped out over the windward side. Rudder blades on cats are designed to pop up if they hit the bottom.
- While the crew holds the cat, the helm lifts the rudder to the full-up position, unhooks the mainsheet from the clew and lets off the downhaul, to depower the sail.

2. Retrieving a cat is the same as launching. You need to lift the bow to push the wheels under the hulls.

3. A cat is surprisingly easy to pull or push with Cat Trax, so long as the surface isn't too steep.

- If you are landing in an onshore wind, consider lowering the mainsail and making the final approach under jib alone.
- Push the wheels under the hulls and secure them to the shrouds on each side with tethers before pulling the cat ashore. If there are waves breaking, help may be required.

Packing up

If you are sailing on sea water, hose the boat down with fresh water before de-rigging and packing it up. Salt can corrode fittings and build up damaging deposits over time.

- Remove the drainage bung in the transom and drain any water in the hull by tipping the boat.
- Let the sails dry before you put them away. Always roll or flake the mainsail and jib, before putting them into a bag.

- Store rudder and daggerboard foils in padded bags for protection.
- Use an overall top cover to protect the boat and prevent it degrading in UV light. Make sure the cover will keep rain out of the cockpit.
- Dinghies in boat parks can get blown over in a gale. When you leave the boat, tie it down securely to ground anchors on either side.

TIP
If there are breaking waves, never stand between the boat and the shore. Even small waves are powerful: the boat may end up on top of you.

Above: **If you have been sailing on the sea, always wash your boat thoroughly with fresh water to get rid of all salt residue.**

Safety skills

Strong wind sailing

Learning to handle strong winds and how to depower the rig are vital skills in the dinghy sailor's armoury.

The size of a dinghy's sails is normally determined by the need for the boat to sail well in light and moderate winds. The downside of this is that they will develop more power than can be easily handled in strong winds, leading to difficulties controlling the boat, including the possibility of repeated capsizes.

Some boats are designed to be easy to recover from a capsize, and are easy to right. However, others are much more difficult to recover, and will sap your energy while doing so. In any case, even the easiest boats to recover will leave you exhausted if you capsize too many times.

Depowering the sails

The flatter the sail, the less power it will develop, so as the wind starts to increase, maximise tension on the halyards, the cunningham and the mainsail clew outhaul. If you're still overpowered, the sails will need to be reefed (see p78–79).

When sailing close-hauled or on a beam reach, the rig can also be depowered by easing the sheets so that the sails flog either fully or partially. Normally it's the mainsheet that is played in this fashion, although in strong gusts the jib sheet will also need to be eased. On a reach or close reach, it's also possible to turn the boat a little towards the wind, to encourage the sails to flap a little, thereby reducing power.

Losing power with the wind behind you

Once the wind direction is aft of the beam, on a broad reach for instance, this tactic no longer works. When you turn up towards the wind, if the boat is already overpowered, the apparent wind increases even more, with a very real risk of spinning the boat into a capsize. The solution is to turn a little away from the wind in the gusts, but not so far that the boat is at risk of gybing. This may feel like the wrong thing to do to start with, but with practice it will become second nature.

There's an easy way for those who are inexperienced to run downwind in strong winds safely – drop the mainsail and continue under jib alone. This should give plenty of power, but will make steering easy and it also reduces the risk of capsize dramatically.

Below: **Flatten the mainsail as much as possible, using the cunningham, outhaul and vang or gnav. Be prepared to spill wind when necessary to keep the boat flat.**

How much wind is too much?

This will vary for every crew, and also for different boats. Hugely skilled and experienced racing sailors may be able to retain control with winds gusting to force 6 or more, with the boats flying at speeds of up to 20 knots – or even 30 for foiling International Moths. These sailors also tend to be very well practised at capsizing, so they are able to take multiple capsizes in their stride, without getting into difficulty.

However, less experienced racers will struggle even in a lot less wind, although with safety cover on hand, and plenty of advice available from fellow racers afterwards, this can be a good way to push your boundaries and gain confidence in strong winds. The first few times beginners sail in a force 4 can be challenging, especially when gybing.

Below: **To depower the sails when the wind is behind you, bear away during the gusts.**

Trim the boat!

If the bow digs into the water in stronger winds, especially when sailing downwind, move your weight further aft. When sailing close-hauled if the boat is heeling too much, raise the centreboard or daggerboard halfway so that the rig has less to 'push' against. This will reduce heel at the expense of increasing leeway.

Right: **The crew move aft to prevent the bow digging into the water in a fresh breeze. However, never let the transom drag if you slow down.**

Reefing

When the wind gets stronger, dinghy sailors need to reduce sail area or sail power to maintain control, keep sailing and avoid capsizes.

Reefing a dinghy

It's possible to reduce sail area by reefing the sails of many learner and recreational dinghies.

Singlehanded dinghies

Dinghies with no shrouds and a luff tube mainsail – such as the Topper or Laser – have a simple reefing system that is dependent on having no battens in the sail.

- Rig the sail with the cunningham attached to tension the luff.
- Then either rotate the mast to roll the sail, or hold the clew and wrap the sail around the mast.
- When the required amount of sail area is left, attach the kicking strap and outhaul and tension the sail, pulling it as flat as possible. The reefed sail shape will be adequate, but not very efficient.

Double-handed dinghies

Dinghies with shrouds can be fitted with a sophisticated 'slab reefing' system, which works by pulling the bottom panel of the mainsail down onto the boom.

Slab reefing is available on many modern recreational dinghies aimed at the family sailing and tuition markets. Good sail shape is maintained, but power is greatly reduced due to the sail being smaller and lower, therefore the boat will tend to heel less, making it both safer and more efficient.

Slab reefing is easy to manage on dry land. It can also be done on the water, but is considerably more difficult. Caution is the best advice – it's much easier to take a reef out when the wind is too light than to put a reef in when it's too strong.

- Start by turning the boat head-to-wind.
- The mainsail is fitted with two reefing lines, which pull down the luff and leech and effectively remove a 'slab' from the bottom of the sail. On more sophisticated systems, a single control line pulls luff and leech lines down together, with the boom held horizontal by a gnav.
- Let go of the mainsheet, ease off the halyard and pull down the luff line until the eye it passes through is pulled down tightly onto the boom. Repeat the process with the line at the leech. Ease off the kicking strap or gnav before re-tensioning the main halyard.
- The reefed 'slab' can be tucked neatly alongside the boom, using ties to hold it in place.

Far left: **The sail of this singlehander can be rolled around the mast and secured by the downhaul to reduce its size.**

Left: **A slab reefing system used to pull down a horizontal slab in the sail.**

Above: **When sailing downwind in strong breezes it's possible to make adequate progress sailing with only the jib and the boat will be very easy to control.**

A traditional reefing method

If a boat with an aft mainsheet arrangement is not set up for slab reefing, it may still be possible to reef the mainsail, using the traditional round-the-boom method. Simply remove the kicking strap, slide the boom from the gooseneck and rotate it three or four times. This will wrap enough sail around the boom to make a noticeable reduction in sail area, although it takes a little practice to achieve a good reefed sail shape. Traditionally, a sailbag was also wrapped into the sail as it was rolled, with the lanyard hanging free so that the boom end of the kicking strap could be attached to it.

Furling jibs

Most dinghies can be sailed under mainsail alone, with the jib furled. This will reduce the power the rig develops and also make the boat easier to handle singlehanded. The drawbacks are that the boat will not point as close to the wind, or sail as fast close-hauled. It may also be more difficult to tack without getting stuck head-to-wind.

Below: **Many dinghies can sail under mainsail alone with the jib furled for easy handling in stronger winds. This dinghy also has a reefable mainsail.**

Changing to a smaller jib

Many older dinghies have a choice of jibs, with a large genoa designed for light wind use, and a smaller, flatter jib for strong winds. It's rarely practical to swap between the two sails once you're on the water, so the most appropriate is selected, based on the weather forecast, when you rig the boat in preparation for sailing.

Above: **With a transom sheeted mainsail it's possible to improvise reefing by rolling the sail around the boom.**

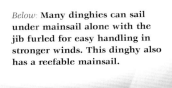

Capsizing: the basics

There can be few dinghy sailors who have never capsized, but once you have mastered sailing, capsizes should become a rare occurrence and recovery will become progressively easier with practice.

There are three problems associated with capsizing:

❂ You will probably get very wet!

❂ You may get cold, unless you are wearing the right clothing for the conditions.

❂ You may get tired, particularly if conditions mean you capsize several times. If that happens, be prepared to signal a rescue boat for help.

Initial action

Get ready to fall in the water as the boat capsizes. You won't need to jump, just slide gracefully

downwards once the deck is at almost 90 degrees to the water. It's important to resist the temptation to hold on to the top of the boat, as this may cause it to invert, making recovery more difficult.

Modern dinghies float high on their sides and blow surprisingly quickly downwind. Therefore you must keep hold of something like the tiller or a sheet when you fall in the water. You may not be able to grab the hull because it is so smooth.

If you become separated from the boat, try to swim back as quickly as possible. If you're sailing

singlehanded and can't catch the boat, indicate you need help by waving your arms above your head. If you are sailing double-handed and one crew becomes separated, it should be possible to right the boat singlehanded, then sail over to pick up the other crew. If not, indicate that you need help in the same way.

Capsize checks

1. As soon as the boat capsizes, check other crew member(s) are okay. Once you have established everyone is safe you can start preparing to right the boat.

Below: **Reaching up to the centreboard or daggerboard can be difficult if the boat floats high.**

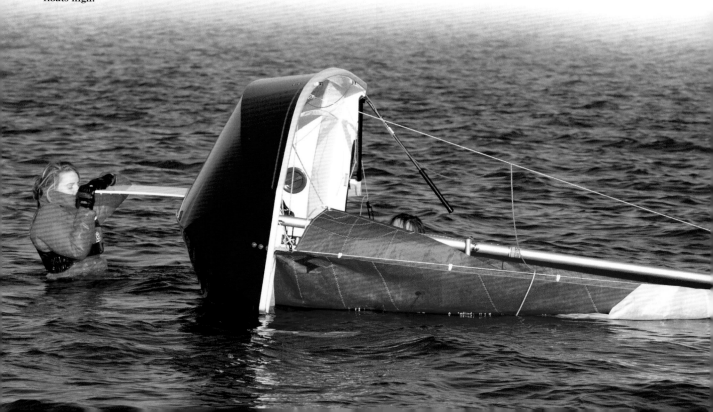

Trapped?

It's possible to get caught under the mainsail when the boat capsizes, or under the hull if the boat inverts. If you're caught under a Dacron mainsail, it is relatively easy to push the material up to get an airspace, before moving out from underneath the sail. Mylar laminate sails are more rigid and less forgiving, but don't panic: just swim or push yourself out past the leech of the sail. If the boat fully inverts you should find an air pocket underneath that will allow you to breathe comfortably.

Right: **Don't hold on to the top of the boat as it capsizes (ie the highest part when it's on its side) – doing so risks pulling it over to a completely inverted position.**

2. Make sure the mainsheet and jib sheet aren't cleated and can run free.

3. Check the centreboard or daggerboard is fully down. This is needed to right the boat, but a loose daggerboard may slide out of its case, and a loose centreboard may swivel back into the hull.

Reaching the daggerboard
Once you have completed all the initial checks, the helm should

Below: **If you capsize with a spinnaker up, you must first stow it in the bag or chute. Unless the wind is very light, you will not be able to right the boat with the spinnaker hoisted.**

swim round to the centreboard/daggerboard, holding the end of the mainsheet. The board may be quite high above the water, but this should be no problem on a small singlehander – grabbing hold of the end of the board may suffice to pull the boat upright. However, on bigger dinghies you will need to climb onto the daggerboard to pull the boat upright.

Once the helm has hold of the board, the crew can throw one of the jib sheets over the top of the boat, which will help the helm climb on top of the board. The helm should stand on the board, toes against the hull, and lean back while holding the jib sheet – or dedicated righting line under the gunwale – for support.

The crew should float in the water near the middle of the boat, so that they are scooped up as the boat comes upright, and can then help the helm on board.

Capsizing: action after recovery

Once both crew are back on board, they must balance the boat, steering up into the wind if necessary with the sails depowered. Check first that there is no damage or missing gear, then set about emptying the water from the cockpit.

Many modern dinghies are designed to hold minimal water after a capsize, so you can sail off immediately while the self-bailers in the cockpit floor drain the water. Boats with a closed transom may have hinged flaps that can be opened to allow the bulk of the water to flow out while sailing fast on a broad reach.

However, some dinghies sail too slowly for self-bailers to work and don't have transom openings. If so, you will need to bail out the water by hand – so remember to always keep a suitable bailer securely attached to the boat.

Exhaustion

In normal circumstances you can capsize and continue sailing, but after righting the boat it's a good time to consider whether you feel okay physically. If you feel at all exhausted, head for the beach before you capsize again. Getting dunked in the water during a capsize will also make you far more vulnerable to the effects of wind chill – if you're feeling cold, that's the time to head home. Similarly, if you keep capsizing, summon help so that you can get a tow back to shore.

Other dangers

If you're sailing in tidal waters, check where the stream is sweeping your capsized boat. In some cases, you may need to right the boat and start sailing as quickly as possible: for instance, if you are being swept into a busy deepwater channel.

Below: **Endless clambering up onto a capsized boat is really tiring. It can be a vicious circle: you get exhausted, therefore you capsize again; you get more exhausted and capsize yet again.**

Be careful if a RIB or powerboat driver offers to help you – if it's not a dedicated safety boat, the driver may not be trained in recovering a dinghy and its crew. Beware of the propeller, which is potentially lethal – check the driver puts the gear shift into neutral (or even better turns the engine off) when anywhere near a person in the water, or the rigging or the sails.

It's important that buoyancy compartments do not leak; if they fill up with water during a capsize, this could sink the boat. They should be tested annually (see p174–5). Many dinghies have one or two drainage plugs in the transom and at the base of each buoyancy tank.

Always check the plugs are pushed or screwed right in before launching the boat. When you pull the boat ashore, remove the plugs and tip the boat up on its trolley to ensure any water is drained.

Below: **Be careful close to a powerboat such as a RIB. The driver must put the gear shift in neutral (or even better, turn the engine off) to ensure the propeller is not turning near to people in the water.**

Below: **Don't lose the boat! Hang on so you can scramble aboard when it comes upright after a strong wind capsize.**

Filling with water

Some dinghies (particularly older designs) have single skin bottoms that do not drain water out of the cockpit. The advantage of this is that the boat should float fairly low in the water when capsized. The disadvantage of this is that when righted, the cockpit may be half full of water.

Below: **There is a lot of water to shift if you capsize a classic dinghy like an Optimist. All you can do is bail like fury.**

Capsizing: dealing with problems

Recovery from a capsize does not always go smoothly. The boat may be difficult to pull back upright, it may keep capsizing or it could turn upside down. These problems can be solved with practice and clear thinking about what to do next.

Above: **Swimming the bow round so that it is pointing towards the wind will make the boat easier to pull upright.**

A capsized dinghy will normally blow downwind of the rig, which acts like a sea anchor. If the boat is difficult to pull upright, one person should swim to the bow and hold it until the boat is pointing into the wind. That should allow the wind to blow under the rig, helping lift it off the water, and as the boat comes upright it should be pointing on a close reach, with the sails flapping.

Rolling back over

Don't pull the boat upright if the wind will blow straight on to the leeward side of the sails – when the wind catches the sail it will capsize the boat in the opposite direction. Instead, swing the bow round into the wind, again with the crew swimming to the bows if necessary. If you are sailing double-handed,

after getting back on board the helm and crew should be prepared to put their weight on both leeward and windward sides of the cockpit as necessary. If you are sailing singlehanded, be ready to throw your weight across the cockpit quickly.

Inversion

Dinghies that float high in the water can turn upside down. This may happen if the crew stands on the rig, which will sink down, or if they cling to the top of the boat as it capsizes, rather than dropping into the water.

If the boat inverts, swim clear. If you are caught underneath the boat, stay calm, find the air pocket underneath and then push yourself down and out to the side. When the boat is upside down it is quite

easy for one crew to climb up on the gunwale and grab the end of the daggerboard. If the crew then leans backwards, the transom will lift, allowing the boat to pivot into the wind as the rig slowly rises towards the surface. When the boat is on its side, resume the normal capsize righting procedure.

Pulling a boat upright

1. If the boat is upside down, make sure the daggerboard or centreboard is fully extended.

2. One crew stands on the gunwale and pulls back – this is enough to float the rig to the surface.

Entrapment

Accidents are extremely rare, but a handful of sailors have drowned after becoming trapped beneath the rig or the boat. Beware of a trapeze harness hook snagging a shroud or control line. This is most unlikely to happen, but the immediate solution is: don't panic, work out the problem and unclip the hook. Even better, if you are wearing a modern harness with a sacrificial hook, you can just pull the release and let it go. If not, undo the release buckle on the side of the harness and wriggle out.

Prevention is better than cure, so make sure all control lines are taut and that there is no excess rope you could get tangled in. Avoid wearing bulky clothes that may snag – a close-fitting buoyancy aid is ideal and makes it much easier to move in the water. Carry a safely secured sharp knife for emergency use.

Below: **Don't panic if you get caught under the sail, or under the boat if it inverts.**

Capsizing to windward

Above: **If your dinghy capsizes to windward, don't panic. Just slide back into the water in the space between the boom and boat, so that you don't end up under the mainsail.**

If you're hiking out or trapezing when the sails suddenly lose power, the boat will roll to windward and may capsize. Look ahead to predict what's going to happen, so you're ready to bear away if the wind heads you, or move into the middle of the boat in a lull.

3. The second crew is ready to stand on the daggerboard in the normal capsize position.

4. He pulls the boat upright while the crew in the water holds on to the bow.

Capsizing: expert recovery

Experienced sailors are able to stay dry in a capsize, climbing over the top of the boat to reach the centreboard. This is both faster and less tiring than the method outlined earlier, but it doesn't always work.

Expert double-handed capsize

Expert sailors know when a capsize is inevitable and, as the boat passes the point of no return, they will already be placing a leg over the upper side of the boat's hull as it goes over. They will then swing their other leg over and slide down the hull to stand on the centreboard.

The window of opportunity for doing this is short – hang on for too long and you will pull the boat over so far it will start to invert. On a two-handed dinghy only one person, normally the helm, can enjoy the luxury of staying dry – the crew is relegated to falling in the water.

The perfect capsize in a singlehander
❂ You know it has become inevitable so, as the rig drops down onto the water, step over the side of the hull onto the centreboard.

❂ Make sure that the mainsheet is uncleated.

❂ Grip the gunwale with both hands and lean back. A small singlehander like a Pico or a Laser will start to right itself immediately.

❂ If the rig doesn't lift off the water, you need more leverage – step further back on the centreboard.

❂ Once the rig has lifted off the water, it will start to lift quite quickly. When it has reached an angle of 45 degrees, be prepared to pop one leg over the deck.

❂ Step over with the other leg as the boat comes upright. If necessary, move your weight rapidly to the other side of the boat to stabilise it.

❂ Get your bearings, and sail away.

The perfect capsize in a double-hander
❂ For the helm, the technique is similar to a singlehander – just step over the side onto the centreboard as the boat capsizes.

❂ The crew should slide gracefully into the water between the mast and the cockpit. Don't fall into the sail and don't hang on to the topsides, as your weight may invert the boat.

❂ As soon as the dinghy has capsized, both crew should check that the other is okay.

Left: **If the boat capsizes to windward you may not have time to climb over the top and onto the centreboard without getting wet.**

Below (left to right): **1. The crew is in the water and the helm checks that she is unhurt. 2. The helm stands on the centreboard and pulls on a righting line. 3. The helm and crew ensure that the mainsail and jib sheet are uncleated and can run free. 4. As the helm rights** the boat, the crew is in the water, ready to be scooped back into the cockpit. **5. As the rig lifts off the water, the helm steps over the side of the dinghy at the same time as the crew rolls into the boat. 6. Helm and crew can now stabilise the boat and sail off.**

❂ Next, ensure both main and jib sheets are uncleated and can run free.

❂ If the spinnaker is hoisted, this must be pulled back inside its chute.

❂ The helm stands on the centreboard, leaning back

by pulling on a righting line – some dinghies have these under the gunwales – or by using a spinnaker sheet or jib sheet.

❂ The crew must be ready to get scooped back into the cockpit, by floating alongside without pulling down on the hull.

❂ As the rig lifts off the water, the crew should roll into the cockpit just before the helm steps in from the other side.

❂ At this point helm and crew are on different sides, perfectly positioned to stabilise the boat and then start sailing again.

Expert sailor's singlehanded capsize

1. If capsize is inevitable, step over the side of the hull onto the centreboard as the rig drops down onto the water. Hold on and get your balance, then check the mainsheet is uncleated.

2. Hold the gunwale with both hands and lean back. A small singlehander will start to right itself, but if the rig does not lift off the water, step further back on the centreboard for more leverage and try again.

3. Once the rig has lifted off the water, it will start to lift quite quickly. When it has reached 45 degrees, be prepared to place one leg over the deck.

4. Quickly step over with the other leg as the boat comes up. If necessary, move rapidly to the other side of the boat to stabilise it. Get your bearings, make sure everything is ready, then sail away.

Capsizing a catamaran

The wide base of a catamaran is a lot more stable than a dinghy at rest, but beach cats can and do capsize – particularly if you're sailing the boat hard and fast.

How do you capsize?

There are two ways a catamaran is likely to capsize. Firstly, it may be blown over sideways like a dinghy. But the crew of a cat have much greater leverage than a dinghy, so this type of capsize is normally easy to prevent by letting go of the mainsheet or traveller.

Secondly, the cat may 'pitchpole'; a typical high-speed cat-sailing capsize. The cat is sailing fast on a reach. The leeward bow drives down into a wave, but does not surface quickly enough to prevent the boat from decelerating. Momentum keeps driving the rig forward, while the apparent wind direction swings behind and increases as the cat decelerates. The leeward bow is driven deeper into the water until the cat tips over and capsizes.

Below: **The point of no return. All you can do is slide gracefully down the trampoline as the cat goes over.**

Below: **Aieeee! Cat capsizes can be fast! Be prepared to be flung off in a pitchpole, like the crew of this Hobie.**

Going over

When a cat capsizes, there is more distance to fall. If possible, both crew should slide down the trampoline into the water; it is best to avoid jumping onto the fully battened sail.

If the cat pitchpoles, the capsize may be fast and quite violent. Both crew will be thrown forwards. Watch out you don't swing round the front of the boat if you are on a trapeze. If this happens, beware of hitting the spinnaker pole – you may damage it or it may damage you!

As an antidote, brace your legs or grab something solid to prevent yourself being thrown forwards.

Capsize checks

In the event of a capsize, remember the following:

☼ First ensure that both crew are OK and not injured.

☼ Do not let go of the capsized cat, which will quickly start to blow downwind. Grab a sheet or control line to maintain contact.

☼ If the mast is sealed the cat should float on its side. Do not stand on the rig; this may invert the boat.

☼ Swim round and climb onto the lower hull. This is normally a lot easier than it might sound!

☼ Both crew can take a rest here, and hold the underside of the trampoline securely.

Getting the cat upright

The width of a cat can make it difficult to pull back upright. The rig, with its elliptical mast, is heavy to lift off the water, and you also need to pull the top hull up to a vertical position.

The cat will naturally blow downwind of its rig, but it is easier to pull the cat back upright with the bows pointing into the wind. This will allow wind to blow under the mast and mainsail. To get the cat into this position, the crew should move forward to sink the bow and lift the stern, thus encouraging the bows to pivot towards the wind.

The big pull

☼ Before you try to pull the cat upright, make sure the mainsheet and jib sheets are uncleated so that they will run free. If the spinnaker is out, it must be pulled back into the chute.

☼ All beach cats should be fitted with a righting line that the crew can grab easily. This line is permanently stowed in its own bag, and tied to the cat platform close to the foot of the mast.

☼ Pull the righting line out of its bag, then throw the free end over the top hull and catch it on the other side. Now lean back and pull. The righting line should be knotted so that it's easy to hold on. To make it easier still, take a turn around your trapeze hook.

☼ In most situations, both crew will need to lean back on the righting line to provide enough leverage to pull the cat upright.

Below **When the cat is on its side, the crew can stand on the lower hull. Note the righting line, which is attached just below the mast base and led over the top hull for the crew to pull back on.**

Capsizing a catamaran (2)

Righting an upturned catamaran

Coming upright

When the rig lifts off the water and the top hull swings past a vertical position, the capsized cat will accelerate through 90 degrees as it swings fully upright.

Watch out for the windward hull as it falls from above and hits the water. You do not want to be under it, but that's easy to avoid. As the windward hull hits the water, both crew should be ready to grab the forward beam to steady the boat, or grab the bar (called a dolphin striker) under the forward beam, which is easier to hold on to.

Getting back on

Most cats have at least one trapeze handle on each side. Use this to pull yourself back onto the trampoline. Swim round the outside of the hull to the windward side. Grab the trapeze handle, lie back in the water, lift your feet onto the deck and pull yourself up. It's easier than it sounds!

Or, you can climb over the back beam, but it can be tricky with the tiller bar in the way. Climbing over the front beam is possible with a dolphin striker as a step, but becomes difficult if the cat starts moving forwards through the water.

Below: **This is the best way to get back on the trampoline. Grab the trapeze handle, put your feet on the side and then pull yourself up.**

Above (left to right): **1. If the cat is upside down, climb onto the upturned trampoline. 2. Lead the righting line over one hull. 3. Pull from the bow, which will pivot the cat and allow the rig to float upwards. 4. Let the cat pivot so it is pointing towards the wind. 5. Take a breather before pulling back hard to lift the rig off the water. 6. As the cat comes upright, prepare to grab the front beam or dolphin striker (the reinforcement strut under the mast). 7. Climb back on board. Well done!**

Upside down

One advantage of an upside down cat is that it will only drift slowly with the wind. Another is that you can sit quite comfortably on the upturned boat and take a rest.

To start getting the cat upright, you first need to pull it up on to its side, so that it is in the normal capsize position.

The procedure for this is:

⊕ Lead the righting line under the deck of the windward bow (nearest the wind) and over the bottom of the hull.

⊕ Take the free end of the righting line towards the bow of the leeward hull (furthest from the wind) so that you can pull diagonally across the bottom of the upturned boat.

⊕ With the leeward bow pushed down, the windward stern will lift off the water and the rig will float towards the surface. Once the cat is on its side, continue to right it in the normal way. This may prove impossible if the mast is stuck on the bottom or the cat has filled with water, in which case

a rescue boat may be required to help pull the cat back upright. Cross both hands above your head to show you need help.

> **TIP**
>
> If the cat inverts, keep clear of the trampoline. If you get caught underneath (which is most unlikely) don't panic. Just push yourself out to the side.

Vital manoeuvres

Being able to manoeuvre back to a person in the water, pick up a mooring or come alongside another boat or a pontoon are important skills. The key to each is stopping the boat, normally by releasing the sheets and turning up into the wind.

Above: **The wind is blowing along this pontoon, allowing the dinghy to lie alongside with the mainsail hoisted. If the wind is blowing on to the pontoon the mainsail must be lowered.**

Man overboard!

While you need to act quickly, the person in the water should be wearing a buoyancy aid and suitable clothing, so it's also important not to panic – make sure the recovery is done in a safe and controlled way.

✪ Keep watching the person's position while you turn the boat – it's easy to lose sight of them.

✪ Turn on to a beam reach the moment the person falls out of the boat.

✪ Tack the boat round to return to the man overboard (MOB).

✪ If possible, furl the jib so that you can control your speed with the mainsail. Make your approach on a close-reaching course, leaving enough space to turn head-to-wind beside them.

✪ Bring the boat to a dead stop, with the person in the water as close as possible to the windward shroud. Take care not to run them over.

✪ The person being rescued may be able to climb over the windward side. Alternatively, they should climb in over the transom.

Overboard from a cat

Catamarans are faster than dinghies, so will cover a greater distance before they can turn around and sail back towards the MOB.

✪ Keep the boat flat on the water and don't risk a capsize.

✪ Keep watching the MOB.

✪ Gybe instead of tack – it's a quicker and more reliable way of turning a cat.

✪ The MOB should climb back onto the windward hull by the shroud. They should lie back in the water, grab the trapeze handle, lift a foot onto the hull and pull up onto the trampoline.

Overboard alone

If you're sailing singlehanded and fall over the side, hang on to the mainsheet and don't let go. The boat will quickly capsize, so then you can pull yourself to the boat and recover from the capsize.

Coming alongside a pontoon

✪ Dinghies are rarely equipped with fenders to protect the hull, so check the pontoon has suitable fendering in place.

✪ Try to approach on a course that allows you to turn head-to-wind in the final approach, and come to a dead stop as you come alongside.

✪ If it's only possible to come alongside on a downwind course, drop the mainsail before making the approach, then furl the jib to slow right down before you come alongside.

Picking up a mooring

✪ Make the final approach at slow speed on a close reach, so that you can bring the dinghy to a stop, with the buoy staying near the windward shroud.

✪ The crew should secure a line to the buoy, either with a bowline or by leading the end of the line back to the boat.

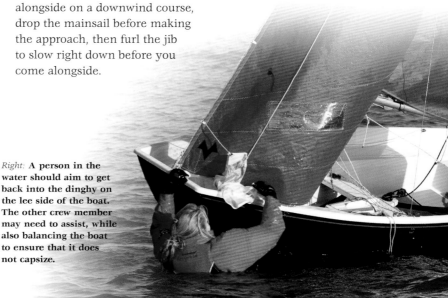

Right: **A person in the water should aim to get back into the dinghy on the lee side of the boat. The other crew member may need to assist, while also balancing the boat to ensure that it does not capsize.**

- Lift the centreboard or the daggerboard and drop the mainsail, so that the boat is stable on the mooring.
- In tidal waters you will need to point the boat in to the direction of the tide to stop. If this means that the wind is behind the boat and the mainsail can't be depowered, sail downtide of the buoy, drop the mainsail and approach under jib alone.

Anchoring

Similar considerations apply to anchoring – once you've identified a suitable sheltered spot, which is clear of other traffic, bring the boat to a stop and gently lower the anchor. The boat will drift away slowly as you do so – this is a good thing as it means the anchor rode will not land on top of the anchor and prevent it from digging into the seabed. Once the anchor is down, check that it's not dragging.

Recommended safety equipment

- A mobile phone in a watertight case. You should also consider carrying a handheld marine VHF in case there is no signal.
- A handheld, waterproof GPS for information on position and speed.
- A safety knife that will cut through rope, shock-cord or trampoline mesh (a folding knife, which can be stowed in the front pocket of a buoyancy aid, is recommended for each crew).
- Extra clothing, including spray jackets, sailing gloves and fleece hats. These should be stowed in a waterproof compartment.
- Water, to prevent dehydration. A water bottle can be attached to the base of the mast, or held by a cage in the cockpit.
- Power food bars for a quick and easily digested energy hit.
- A small pack of flares for use in inland or coastal waters.

- One or two paddles in case of light winds.
- A towline at least 10m (33ft) long.
- Basic tools, including pliers and a shackle key. A Leatherman or Gerber-style stainless steel multi-tool could be very useful. Make sure it is attached to the boat!

Making a pickup

Try to keep watching the man overboard as you tack to head back on a reach to a point downwind of the person in the water. Aim to turn upwind so the boat will come to a dead stop, head-to-wind, with the person overboard by the windward shroud, where you can grab them or they can hold the boat. Depending on your level of sail control, you may need to furl the jib or let it flap on the final approach.

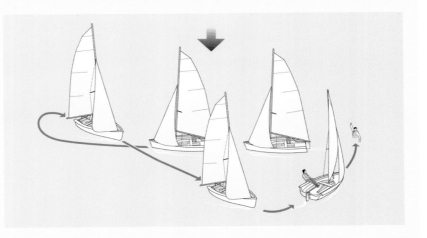

Performance sailing/racing

Using a trapeze

Trapezing allows you to stand out on the side of the boat, suspended by a wire, so that you can use maximum leverage to hold the boat upright. What's more, it's nothing like as difficult as it looks!

The trapeze harness

The trapeze harness should be comfortable, fitting snugly over your wetsuit or drysuit, but under your buoyancy aid, which should be cut high to leave room for the hook. Beware of old harnesses without a 'sacrificial hook' that allows you to press a button or pull a lanyard to detach it if the hook becomes snagged when you're in the water after capsizing.

Most harnesses have 'spreader bars', to spread the pull from the wire across your hips. These are adjusted with straps, which have quick-release buckles so you can undo them in a hurry. Some harnesses have a hook on a central plate laced to each side – these are more fiddly to put on, but can be more comfortable. If you want to trapeze in high-performance, flat-out fashion, a harness with full back support is needed.

Practising a trapeze

Capsizing on the trapeze

Don't be afraid of capsizing – stay cool, unhook as soon as you know capsize is inevitable and get off the side.

1. Crouch down as the boat goes over, unhook from the ring and then slide down the outside of the hull.

2. Get your weight off the side as soon as possible to avoid fully inverting the boat, but try not to fall forwards onto the sail.

3. If the boat capsizes to windward on top of you, concentrate on getting the hook off the trapeze ring. If you are under the mainsail, get out by moving towards the stern of the boat.

Trapezing height

Trapeze wires are attached to the mast on each side of the boat. Each wire has a stainless steel 'ring', which holds the hook. When not in use, each wire and ring is held taut by shock-cord attached to the deck or trampoline.

Trapeze rings can normally be adjusted for height, using a short control line – the lower you trapeze, the more effective your leverage will be. However, it's easier to learn with the ring set high. It can be useful to adjust the height of the ring while sailing, pulling the ring higher so that your body clears the waves, or lowering the ring when you move aft on a broad reach.

Going out on the wire

The best conditions for learning to trapeze are flat water with a steady wind around force 3 – lighter, gusty winds make trapezing difficult. You

Above: **A harness is fitted to the body over your wetsuit and under your buoyancy aid.**

want enough power to go out on the wire without fear of pulling the boat over to windward. To go out on the wire:

✪ Sit on the side of the boat, with your feet tucked under the toe straps.

Below (left to right): **1.** Sit on the side and pull the trapeze ring on to the hook. **2.** Hold the trapeze handle with your back hand, take your weight on the wire and step out on the back foot. Follow with the front foot and try to relax. **3.** Straighten both legs slightly to get body weight away from the boat and let go of the handle. **4.** Keep your feet slightly apart with legs flexed. **5.** Holding the jib or spinnaker sheet helps balance. Bend your legs if the wind drops and the boat heels to windward. **6.** Crouch as you come back in. **7.** Drop both feet back on to the cockpit floor then take the trapeze ring off and let it go on its shock-cord.

- ✪ Hold the handle above the trapeze ring with your front hand, and slip the ring on to the hook with your back hand.
- ✪ Sit back in a semi-hiking position, taking any slack off the trapeze wire. If it is still slack, adjust the ring to a higher position so it can't fall off the hook.
- ✪ Make sure the boat is well powered up, so that it will take your weight on the wire without rolling to windward.
- ✪ Hold the jib sheet with your back hand and move your body out, taking the weight on the trapeze wire as you swing your front foot onto the side of the boat.
- ✪ Step out with your back foot, pushing off the side with your back hand into a crouched position, with both feet on the side of the boat.
- ✪ Straighten your legs with your feet close together. Keep your front leg straight and your back leg slightly bent to stop yourself falling forward.

Coming in off the wire
- ✪ Bend both legs so that you're in a crouched position, and grab the trapeze handle with your front hand.
- ✪ Slip your back foot into the cockpit, supporting your body with your back hand.

- ✪ Follow with your front foot, so that you're sitting on the side of the boat in a semi-hiking position.
- ✪ Knock the trapeze ring off the hook and let go of the handle.

Expert trapezing

Good technique allows you to progress to the fastest boats on the water, on which both helm and crew can trapeze at the same time. Start by learning to relax on the trapeze and keep your balance at all times.

Best trapezing technique

- ✪ Stand with the balls of your feet on the side of the boat. Face forwards. Keep your feet together.
- ✪ The trapeze wire will pull you forwards, particularly if you move back when the boat is sailing on a reach. Use your front leg as a brace, with your back leg slightly bent to adjust your balance.
- ✪ As soon as you are out on the wire, let go of the handle. The wire will hold your weight.
- ✪ Keep hold of the jib sheet – it helps your balance if it's taut.
- ✪ As crew, if you lose your balance,

grab the helmsman's buoyancy aid so you don't swing forwards.
- ✪ Stand by the shroud when beating upwind. Move aft when the boat bears away on to a reach, stepping back along the side of the boat and keeping your front leg braced against increased forward pull from the wire.
- ✪ If waves keep hitting your body, pull the trapeze ring to a higher position, so that a wave can't knock your feet off the boat.

Rolling to windward

Having a crew out on the wire provides a lot of leverage, so if there is a lull in the wind, the boat will roll to windward. The crew on the trapeze must anticipate this and react by bending their legs into a semi-crouched position, or coming right in off the trapeze.

In marginal winds it is fairly easy for the crew to push weight in or out, with the helm keeping his or her weight steady and concentrating on keeping power in the sails.

Trapezing on a catamaran

Catamarans are more stable than dinghies, which make them excellent boats to learn to trapeze on. However, there's nothing for your feet to push

Below: **Trapezing on a spinnaker reach in a force 3. Note the way the crew keeps his feet close together, leaning aft and looking forward.**

Below: **Helming a dinghy from the wire is a balancing act, particularly when sailing on a broad reach. Note how this singlehander stands right on the stern to lift the bows while the boat is planing.**

Top: **Best practice is to keep your feet close together like the helm of this catamaran is doing, not like the crew who appears to be a bit wobbly.**

Bottom: **When sailing a catamaran, use weight on the trapeze so the windward hull is skimming the surface. It's easier for the crew to go in and out, while the helm stays out on the wire.**

against on the flat trampoline or windward deck, so moving out on to the trapeze requires a committed push with your back hand.

A cat can accelerate very quickly; brace your back leg to counteract this. Sudden deceleration is likely to pose bigger problems, because if the leeward bow drives into a wave the cat will slow suddenly, throwing the crew forwards. In the worst case, the crew will slingshot around the front of the boat, which can lead to a capsize, and bruises!

A slingshot is most likely to happen on a reach, when the crew has moved right to the stern of the windward hull to keep the leeward bow flying. You need a dynamic posture, facing forwards with the front leg straight and braced and the back leg well bent.

If you're trapezing while crewing, grab the helmsman for support if you start to fly forwards. Some cats have a foot strap to anchor the crew's back foot by the rear beam. Others have a 'retaining line' with a small hook, which connects the end of the beam to the crew's trapeze ring to stop him being thrown forwards.

Twin wiring

Some high-performance dinghies and many cats have twin trapezes. The crew should trapeze lower, providing the helm with a clear view forwards. Sailing upwind, both crew go out on the wire and stand close together. The technique for moving out and coming back in on the trapeze is similar for helm and crew: step out with the front foot first, and then follow immediately with the back foot. The helm has to maintain control of the rudder at the same time.

As you go out or in on the wire, 'lock' the rudder in the straight-ahead position by pushing the tiller extension down hard with your back hand on the side of the boat. With both crew on the wire, it can be a big help if the crew takes the mainsheet when sailing upwind. The helm can concentrate on steering the boat, the crew can use both hands to trim the sheet and, that way, the boat keeps sailing flat at full speed.

Sailing with a spinnaker

Dinghies may have a symmetric or asymmetric spinnaker for use when sailing on a reach or a run. Both have advantages, although the more modern asymmetric is simpler to use. In both cases they greatly increase boat speed – and excitement!

Asymmetric versus symmetric

Until the early 1980s, when the asymmetric shape was developed, all dinghy spinnakers were symmetrical in shape, with both vertical sides (luffs) the same length. The symmetric spinnaker looks like a puffed-up triangle, with the windward corner set from a pole attached to the mast.

It is designed primarily for sailing downwind and is extremely effective on a dead run with the pole pulled back against the shroud. It can also be flown on a close reach with the pole against the forestay.

The symmetric spinnaker is excellent for inland waters where sailing space may be limited, and it's much more efficient when sailing directly downwind, although you still have the option of reaching. However, it's a demanding sail to master: rewarding if you get everything right, but unforgiving if you get anything wrong.

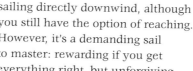

Below: **Symmetric spinnakers can be a lot of fun, and are good for restricted areas of water.**

Asymmetric benefits

The asymmetric spinnaker is at its best on open water where you can enjoy a high-speed blast without any worries about running out of space while gybing downwind. The asymmetric spinnaker resembles an oversized jib, has three sides of different lengths and is flown from the end of a pole that sticks straight out from the bows.

Unlike the symmetric spinnaker, it only has one clew, which allows the crew to sheet the sail on either side, while the pole remains in position.

Asymmetric spinnakers are designed for sailing at full bore on a reach, with the power providing increased speed, which in turn increases the apparent wind.

They are not designed for running straight downwind, although some asymmetric dinghies are fitted with a spinnaker pole that can be angled to the windward side to improve downwind performance. Large asymmetric spinnakers are not good on a close reach, when there will be too much power in the sail.

> **TIP**
>
> The halyard is pulled through a cleat, which will jam automatically. Hoist the spinnaker on land and once it is fully up, mark the halyard where it passes through the cleat. Then, every time you hoist on the water, you will know when the spinnaker is fully up.

Safe hoisting and dropping

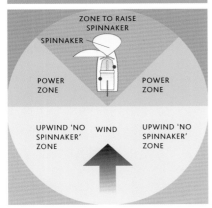

When the wind is astern of the dinghy there is least pressure on the spinnaker. As soon as the boat moves on to a broad reach, you move into a zone where the spinnaker will catch the wind and power up. Do not hoist or drop the spinnaker in this zone if at all possible.

Spinnaker care

Spinnakers are made from lightweight, rip-stop nylon, which will tear if it snags. Make sure sharp items such as split pins, rings or shackles are well covered with insulating tape. When recovering the sail, don't pull hard if it snags – look for the cause of the problem. Use spinnaker tape to repair small tears. It's readily available and sticks easily to a dry, clean sail with all salt removed.

The asymmetric spinnaker is easy to master, as long as you learn with one of modest size, which will be relatively forgiving.

Capsizing with a spinnaker set

Follow the same procedure as outlined on p80–1. However, the extra windage on the sail will make righting the boat harder and it may be more difficult to control once it's upright. Therefore, before righting the boat, the crew should pull the sail back into its chute or bag.

Below: **Skiffs with big asymmetric spinnakers can be extremely fast. They tend to sail downwind in a series of zigzags which generates additional apparent wind.**

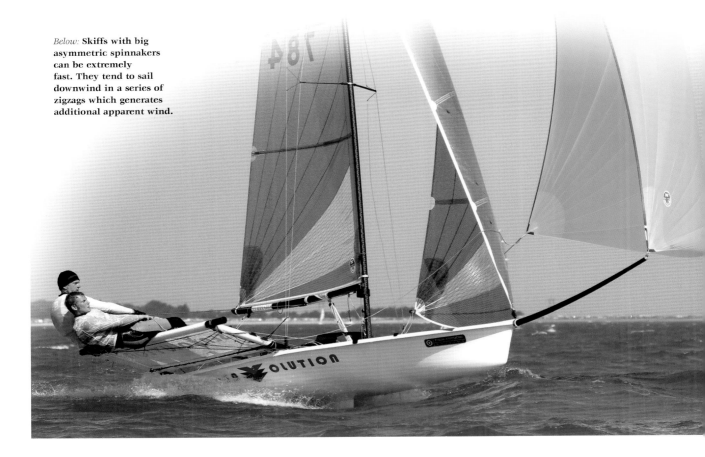

Asymmetric basics

Unlike the mainsail or jib, the spinnaker is a free-flying sail, which is hoisted and dropped while you are sailing at speed. When setting up the spinnaker, it's vital to ensure you've got everything right.

Setting up an asymmetric spinnaker

- Identify the tack, clew and head.
- Use bowlines to attach the halyard, retrieval and tack lines.
- The spinnaker is launched and retrieved using a continuous loop rope. One end is attached to the head of the sail and acts as the halyard, the other is attached to a patch on the outside of the sail, which acts as the retrieval line. The retrieval end of the rope is led through one or two rings on the outside of the sail, which helps feed the sail into the mouth of the chute when it's pulled down.
- The tack of the spinnaker is attached to the tack line at the end of the spinnaker pole.
- The spinnaker sheet also forms a continuous loop. Double it over and push the end of the loop through the ring in the clew, then pull the two free ends through

to lock the sheet tight. Lead the free ends outside the shrouds and through the spinnaker blocks, in the correct direction so that the ratchet on the block locks with the sheet under tension. Tie the two ends of the sheet together with a double figure-of-eight.
- Before going afloat, check the spinnaker can be launched and retrieved successfully. Only the head and clew should be visible when the sail is pulled back into its chute.
- Check that the spinnaker can be gybed from side to side: the sheet must pass outside the jib luff and spinnaker retrieval line. Attention to detail is vital.

Launching an asymmetric spinnaker

Unless the wind is very light, the helmsman must bear away downwind to hoist the spinnaker,

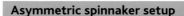

1. Hoist the asymmetric spinnaker to make sure that halyard, retrieval line and sheets are correctly attached and will launch on the correct sides of the shrouds and forestay.

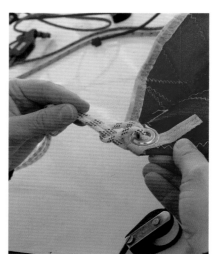

Above: Attaching the middle of the spinnaker sheet to the clew of the sail. Pull the two free ends through to lock the sheet tight.

Left: The helmsman steers deep downwind on a broad reach, ensuring the mainsail blankets the spinnaker while it is being hoisted by the crew.

2. If all is well, use the retrieval line to pull the spinnaker inside its chute.

3. The spinnaker sheet should be continuous, attached to the clew with an overhand knot at the halfway point.

4. The free ends of the sheet should be tied together with a secure double knot so you can grab the sheet at any point.

blanketing it behind the mainsail. This ensures there is no danger of the partly hoisted spinnaker filling with wind and overpowering the boat.

- Bear away downwind, then sail a straight course with the boat absolutely level.
- Make sure the sheets will run free. When the helm is ready for the hoist, the crew stands behind the halyard, pulling it up hand-over-hand as quickly as possible, so that the sail can't drop into the water or fill with wind when it is half-hoisted. With an asymmetric spinnaker the pole

is deployed automatically as the sail is hoisted.
- Take the leeward spinnaker sheet and start to pull it in as the helm heads up on to a broad reach to power up the sail. If the sail is twisted, a gybe may set it straight.

Dropping an asymmetric spinnaker

- Bear away downwind so the crew can get to the middle of the cockpit to release the halyard and pull in the retrieval line, with the mainsail blanketing the spinnaker for maximum control.
- The crew can pass the spinnaker sheet to the helmsman or just stand on it – with the boat sailing downwind, there won't be much power in the sail.
- Pull in any slack on the retrieval line and make sure the continuous halyard/retrieval line cannot snag. Flick the halyard out of its cleat to release it, then quickly pull in the retrieval line.

- If the spinnaker won't pull back all the way into its chute, or it drops into the water and gets run over by the boat, it can lead to a nasty mess, with the spinnaker wrapped round the daggerboard.
- Always tension the retrieval line before the drop: the quicker you pull the retrieval line, the less chance there is of the spinnaker dropping under the boat. Throw both hands back behind your body as you pull the line in.
- Check you're not standing on the halyard/retrieval line, or that the halyard hasn't locked back into its cleat.
- If the spinnaker will not pull into the chute, pulling harder may rip the sail. It's better to quickly re-hoist then drop the spinnaker again.

TIP

Always do a test hoist on dry land when the wind is light. And check the spinnaker is the correct way up – it's embarrassing to hoist it upside down!

Using an asymmetric spinnaker

Learning to launch an asymmetric spinnaker and sail at full bore on the apparent wind, under control, is a matter of avoiding common mistakes.

Sailing on the apparent wind

✪ Asymmetric spinnakers are powerful sails – you need to find the right balance between generating maximum power and maintaining control. This will provide the best VMG (velocity made good) as you sail downwind.

✪ Push the tiller away to steer towards the wind and power up the spinnaker, so that you are sailing at full speed on the apparent wind.

✪ The boat will only respond to steering with an asymmetric when it is kept flat. If the boat heels, it will slow and spin up towards the wind, out of control. When a gust hits and the boat starts to heel, bear away quickly to hold it flat on the water. If the wind drops and the boat slows down, head up to increase power and speed. The wind is never constant in speed or direction, so you will always sail a 'wiggly' course with an asymmetric spinnaker: luffing to build power, bearing away to keep control.

Perfect trim

✪ Sailing downwind with an asymmetric spinnaker, both helm and crew should move well back, especially in moderate and strong winds. Hold the spinnaker sheet with both hands and watch the luff carefully. Pull the sheet in to stop the sail flapping, and then ease it until the luff begins to curl. This will provide maximum power. If there is no curl in the luff, the sail is too tight, which will stall the airflow. If the luff is collapsing, the sail is too loose and power is being lost.

✪ The crew needs to trim the spinnaker sheet virtually all the time. The helm must steer to follow the spinnaker, luffing when power decreases, bearing away when power increases.

Gybing an asymmetric

The great thing about asymmetric spinnakers is that they are very easy to gybe as you blast at full speed downwind, going from gybe to gybe. It's just a matter of thinking clearly, steering carefully, staying on a downwind course and holding the boat flat throughout the turn.

✪ The helmsman should keep the boat as flat as possible throughout the gybe, while concentrating on steering through a steady turn.

Gybing an asymmetric spinnaker

1. Note how the boat is kept flat as the helm bears away dead downwind and the crew pulls in slack on the spinnaker sheet for the new gybe.

2. As the boat changes direction past dead downwind – with wind over the stern and just on the port side – the helm flips the boom across with a yank on the falls of the mainsheet.

- Keep the boat moving fast to minimise apparent wind, which will reduce power in the mainsail. For instance, if you sail through a gybe at 10 knots in 20 knots of true wind, the apparent wind will be 10 knots as it swings behind the boat. But if you slow down to 5 knots, the apparent wind will increase to 15 knots and make the mainsail more difficult to control.
- Beware of luffing too high on the new tack when the mainsail changes sides – be ready to bear away to keep the boat heading downwind and under control, before luffing to build power in the spinnaker.

Crew tasks in a gybe

- Pull the sheet in tight so the sail is against the jib – this will help keep it under control.
- As the helmsman steers into the gybe, grab the new sheet, pulling

Above: **Loads of power and speed on a force 5 day. You can see the helm is bearing away on the apparent wind, heading deeper downwind to keep the boat upright in a gust. If the boat heels any more, it may luff out of control, or 'broach'.**

in any slack. Hold the old sheet as you move across the boat, to help flatten the spinnaker as the stern passes through the wind.

- Let go of the old sheet and quickly pull in the new one as you move

on to the side of the boat, ready to power up for the new reach.

- Trim the spinnaker sheet until the luff has a slight curl. Focus on getting the trim correct.

Below: **The spinnaker helps lift the bow on a flat-out reach. The furled jib decreases sail area and allows clear air to flow into the spinnaker.**

3. Perfect! Keep steering downwind with the boat held flat, letting the crew sheet in on the new side before luffing on to a new reaching course.

Symmetric spinnakers

The classic style of spinnaker is more difficult to manage than the modern asymmetric and practice is needed to keep it under control, particularly in stronger winds.

Setting up a symmetric spinnaker

✿ Identify the head. Run your hand down the port (red) and starboard (green) sides of the sail to ensure each clew is on the correct side of the boat.

✿ If the dinghy is fitted with a spinnaker chute, a continuous loop is used as the halyard and the retrieval line.

✿ Attach one end of the sheet to the starboard clew with a bowline. Lead it back, outside the starboard shroud, through the starboard spinnaker block, and finally across to the port-side spinnaker block. Take the free end forwards outside the port shroud, and tie it to the port clew with a bowline.

✿ Pull the spinnaker into the chute, then check to ensure it can be hoisted and retrieved successfully. The pole isn't connected until immediately

before the spinnaker is hoisted. It is stored alongside the main boom, from where it can be pushed forward by the crew.

Managing the pole

The crew handles the spinnaker pole during hoists, gybes and drops. The pole is attached in three places:

✿ The outer end is clipped on to the 'guy', which acts as the sheet on the windward side of the boat.

✿ The inner end is clipped on to the mast.

✿ The centre is attached to the uphaul/downhaul, which is used to control the pole's vertical angle.

Hoisting the spinnaker

If you launch the spinnaker from a chute in front of the jib, it can be hoisted on either tack. If you launch from a bag in the cockpit, you can

Spinnaker bags and chutes

Most modern dinghies and cats have a 'chute' from which to launch and recover the spinnaker. On some dinghies, however, the spinnaker is stowed in a bag at the front of the cockpit and there is no retrieval line – when lowering the sail the crew has to grab the sail and bundle it into the bag.

only do so on the leeward side, where the mainsail will blanket it.

✿ Slide the spinnaker pole forward from the boom and clip the outer end to the guy. Attach the uphaul/downhaul to the middle of the pole, then clip the inner end to the mast.

✿ The helmsman stands with the tiller between his legs, then pulls up the halyard quickly with both hands, with the crew ready to pull in on the sheet and guy as soon as the spinnaker is fully hoisted.

Above: **The crew attaches the inner end of the spinnaker pole to the mast, while the helm stands with the tiller between his legs – a great position to keep the boat balanced.**

Left: **The symmetric spinnaker requires greater skills than the asymmetric, owing to having a removable pole and a sheet/guy led to each lower corner of the sail.**

Gybing a spinnaker

1. Going into a gybe, the crew unclips the spinnaker pole from the mast, then clips it to the new guy.

2. The crew unclips the end of the pole from the old guy and prepares to clip it to the mast.

3. The helm flips the boom across, the crew pulls back on the guy, until the pole is at the correct angle and starts trimming the sheet.

Trimming the spinnaker

- Adjust the guy so that the pole is roughly at right angles to the wind, with the pole end pressing against the clew of the sail.
- Set the pole height so that both windward and leeward clews are level. This changes with wind angle: the pole needs to be raised for a reach and lowered for a run.
- Cleat the guy and trim the sail using the sheet – for top power the luff should be just curling.
- When sailing on a reach, a hook or 'twinning' line is used to pull the guy down to deck level, next to the windward shroud.

Gybing the spinnaker

The key is to move the pole from side to side, while the boat is sailing almost directly downwind, after the mainsail boom has swung across to the new side.

- Unclip the pole from the mast.
- Clip the end of the pole to the old sheet (this becomes the new guy).

- Unclip the other end of the pole. The old guy will fall away, ready to take over as the new sheet.
- As the wind starts to blow from the new side, the helm flips the boom across. The crew pulls back on the guy, ensuring the pole is at the correct angle and height for the new course, then starts trimming the sheet.
- The crew clips the free end of the pole to the mast, then moves to balance the boat, sheeting in at the same time.

Dropping the spinnaker

Sail deep downwind so that the spinnaker is blanketed. If the boat has a chute, you should release the halyard and pull smartly on the retrieval line, then unclip and stow the pole.

If the boat has a bag in the cockpit, the drop is easiest on the windward side. Take off the pole, then pull the spinnaker down by its leech and bundle it into the bag.

Above: **Some boats have a spinnaker bag by the mast. This keeps weight and complexity out of the bows, but requires greater crew skill when launching or stowing the spinnaker.**

Dinghy and catamaran racing

Racing is fun. It is also the best way to improve sailing ability and make friends at the same time. You can race at all levels, from complete novice to full-time professional.

Where should I race?

Racing is organised by sailing clubs and dinghy classes. Clubs organise local race series for their members, mostly on weekends and summer evenings, plus regattas. Class associations organise regional and national events and championships, where the sailors race at different venues hosted by a local club.

Above: **Turning round the leeward mark on a windward-leeward course. The leading boat has gybed round and is starting to beat back up the course; the pursuing boat has just dropped its spinnaker in the final approach to the mark.**

How should I race?

Boats frequently race together as a class: whoever finishes first is the winner. Different classes may also race together on handicap. In the UK, for instance, a handicap based on past performance of different boats, known as the Portsmouth Yardstick, is widely used for dinghy racing. Catamarans use a handicap based on boat measurements.

Left: **Racing can be crowded! These tightly bunched International Cadets show why it is vital to get clean wind – the boat on the right will be sailing in very disturbed air.**

What should I race?

- Hiking dinghies need less space and are excellent for racing on inland waters where their manoeuvrability provides great tactical racing.
- Trapeze dinghies need space to show off their pace so ideally need larger lakes or the open sea.
- Skiff-style dinghies need even more space for their asymmetric spinnakers, zigzagging in a series of gybes downwind.
- Catamarans need the most space. They are slow to tack or manoeuvre, but very fast in a straight line. They must also sail a zigzag course downwind.

Below: **Insurance cover is required to enter a race. With fast closing speeds, accidents are possible though injuries are rare.**

The race course

A race should ideally test sailors on different points of sailing: upwind, downwind, reaching and mark rounding. A local club may set a course using existing buoys and channel markers. However, for a championship or national event, the organisers will set a course using temporary buoys, using a specified layout. These buoys or marks need to be rounded in a certain order.

Windward–leeward course

The simplest type of course has upwind (windward) and downwind (leeward) legs, with racers sailing a number of times around the course. The start line is at the leeward end of the course and also acts as the finish. A spacer leg with a short beam reach is often incorporated to prevent collisions when boats turn round the windward mark at the top of the course.

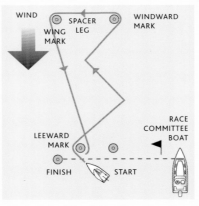

WINDWARD–LEEWARD COURSE

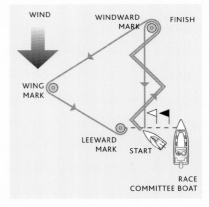

CLASSIC COURSE

Classic course

The traditional Olympic racing course was a 'triangle and sausage' incorporating a beat to the windward mark at the top of the course, a reach out to the 'wing mark', a reach on the opposite gybe to the leeward mark at the bottom of the course, a beat to the windward mark, a dead run to the leeward mark and a final beat to the finish by the windward mark. The sequence of triangles or sausages can be changed, as can the number of laps. Modern variations include the 'P'-shaped or trapezoid course, which can be tailored to provide a suitable mixture of beating, reaching and running.

Racing rules

While the rules of the road state which boat has the right of way in order to avoid collisions on the water, more specific rules are used between boats that are racing.

Watch out!

There is a greater risk of collision at several stages of the race:

- ❂ Boats will be very close together at the start, when they jockey to get away ahead of everyone else.
- ❂ Boats will be crossing on different tacks when sailing upwind towards the windward mark.
- ❂ Boats will be crossing on different gybes when sailing downwind towards the leeward mark.
- ❂ Boats will be squeezed together when rounding marks.
- ❂ Boats will be overtaking on reaches.

Below: **As with any sailing situation, port tack must give way to starboard tack. In this instance, the port tack boats are all clear ahead of the starboard tack one in the foreground.**

Racing rules

The Racing Rules of Sailing are updated by ISAF (the International Sailing Federation) every four years.

If you break a rule (for instance, not giving way on port tack or barging in when turning round a mark), you must do a 'penalty turn' as soon as possible. The penalty turn must be through 360 degrees, requiring a tack and a gybe. Some race organisers require a 720-degree penalty turn.

If you break a rule and continue racing without a penalty turn, another boat may protest. A protest committee will decide the outcome, which may be disqualification.

Right of way

- ❂ *Rule 10: When boats are on opposite tacks, a port tack boat shall keep clear of a starboard tack boat.*

The port tack boat can either tack, slow down or bear away under the stern of the starboard tack boat. This also applies when sailing downwind – the port tack boat must gybe out of the way.

Above: **Boats that have an overlap to windward must keep clear. Here the boat with the blue and white sail cannot bear down on the boats to leeward.**

- ❂ *Rule 11: When boats are on the same tack and overlapped, a windward boat shall keep clear of a leeward boat.*

An 'overlap' is when any part of one boat overlaps the other: for example, when the bow of one boat is level with the helmsman of the other boat. A boat that is attempting to overtake on the windward side cannot force the leeward boat to change course.

- ❂ *Rule 12: When boats are on the same tack and not overlapped, a boat clear astern shall keep clear of a boat clear ahead.*

'Clear astern' or 'clear ahead' means that there is no overlap between the boats.

Key racing rules

Tacking

☼ *Rule 13: After a boat passes head-to-wind, she shall keep clear of other boats until she is on a close-hauled course. During that time rules 10, 11 and 12 do not apply. If two boats are subject to this rule at the same time, the one on the other's port side or the one astern shall keep clear.*

This rule deals with the problem of a port tack boat that tacks (or gybes) at the last moment to avoid a starboard tack boat, with the result that the starboard tack boat has to take avoiding action. The port tack boat must complete its tack and be sailing with the mainsail sheeted in on the new side, while it is in clear water.

Avoiding contact

☼ *Rule 14: A boat shall avoid contact with another boat if reasonably possible...*

Even if you have right of way, avoid collisions at all costs!

Marks or obstructions

☼ *Rule 18: When boats are overlapped the outside boat shall give the inside boat mark-room...*

This rule is used to avoid collisions when boats pile around a mark on the course.

Left: **Tack or dip? In a port-starboard situation, you have to decide if it's best to tack or bear away a few degrees to dip under the stern of the starboard tack boat.**

An overlap must be established before the boats reach the 'three boat length zone', which extends in a circle three boat lengths from the mark. So, basically, you cannot push in at the last moment – you have to wait your turn to round the mark. However, if a boat on the inside establishes an overlap before the three boat length zone, the outside boats must give it enough room to round the mark.

Below: **At this turning mark the two cats must leave space for the two dinghies, which were first to arrive within three boat lengths of the mark.**

Starting a race

Making a perfect start is one of the most important requirements for success, and needs experience and a cool head.

The start line

The race organisers lay a start line, positioning their committee boat at one end to start the race and an outer limit mark at the other end.

The first leg of the race is normally directly upwind. This theoretically gives all boats the chance of an equal start as the wind is coming from ahead.

The length of the start line should be approximately equal to the length of all the boats added together, plus an additional 25–50 per cent to provide a little more space. The start line should be set almost at right angles to the wind, the port end ideally angled forwards by 5–10 degrees.

Hare and tortoise

A Pursuit Race can provide a lot of fun for a fleet with a mixture of different boats. Handicaps are calculated in advance over a specific timescale during which the boats will race round the course. The slowest boats start first, followed by progressively faster boats, with the fastest boats starting last of all. At the end of the period, the race is completed when the leading boat finishes its lap of the course.

This 'line bias' helps to ensure that boats are spread out along the full length of the line at the start. It is extremely difficult to set the start line at a perfect angle to give everyone an equal chance, particularly if the wind keeps changing direction. Too much bias to port, and boats will be able to sail across the fleet on port tack. Too much bias to starboard means all the boats will be bunched up at the starboard end, trying to squeeze around the committee boat, with the rest of the line empty.

Countdown to the start

You need a countdown timer synchronised with the 'warning signal' to make a perfect start. Wear it on your wrist or attach it to the mast or boom, to give both crew and helm a clear view.

- *Warning:* One sound signal. Five minutes to go. The class flag is hoisted on the committee boat.
- *Preparatory:* One sound signal. Four minutes to go. Code Flag P is hoisted (the 'Blue Peter' with blue background and a white square).
- *One minute:* One long sound signal. One minute to go. Code Flag P is dropped.
- *Start:* One sound signal. The class flag is dropped.

The perfect start

The bow of your boat hits the line as the starting signal sounds. Your boat is sailing in the correct direction, at full speed, in clean wind. You have assessed port and starboard bias and worked out which end of the line is most favourable, ensuring you cross at the optimum point.

Right: **Competitors waiting for the outer distance mark to be positioned, to ensure the start line is at the correct angle, prior to a Topper World Championship race on Lake Garda.**

Above: **Catamarans line up for the start of the Eurocat event in France. They are all getting ready to sheet in and make a sprint for the line, just a few seconds before the starting gun.**

The imperfect start

Your boat is boxed in with boats ahead and to windward, which means that the air you are sailing in is disturbed. The result is your boat cannot sail fast or point high – tack as soon as possible to get away from other boats and find clean wind.

Below: **Perfect! Leave the start line at full speed, with no boat ahead or directly to windward. The green boat is well away.**

The premature start

Do not cross the line too early. If any part of your boat is over the line when the starting signal sounds, you are 'on the course side', known as OCS. You must go back and recross the line, without interfering with other boats. The committee boat will signal one or more boats are OCS by making one sound signal and hoisting Code Flag X (blue cross on white background).

Countdown flags

Learn to recognise the flags that identify the countdown to the start. Sound signals are referred to as guns, although normally a horn or whistle is used. Sound signals are used to draw your attention to the flags, which tell you what to do.

CLASS FLAG UP

WARNING: 5 MINUTES

CLASS FLAG AND BLUE PETER UP

PREPARATORY: 4 MINUTES

BLUE PETER DOWN AT 1 MINUTE, THEN CLASS FLAG DOWN AT START

READY TO GO: 0 MINUTES

Flag signals

Sometimes half the fleet or more is over the start line. The committee boat will signal:

⚙ *A General Recall* with two sound signals and the First Substitute flag. All boats must return and wait for the race to be restarted.

⚙ If there are further general recalls, more draconian rules may be used.

⚙ *Round the Ends rule*: Any boat that is OCS within one minute of the start must go round the end of the start line to restart. This is indicated by Code Flag I.

⚙ *Black Flag*: Any boat that is OCS within one minute of the start is disqualified.

PREPARATORY (BLUE PETER)

GENERAL RECALL

POSTPONEMENT

ABANDONED

DISQUALIFIED

ROUND THE ENDS RULE APPLIES

INDIVIDUAL RECALL

PROTEST

Racing round the course

A series of legs lead around the course, which include beating, running and possibly reaching, with windward and leeward turning marks at either end.

Below: **A big fleet crosses the start line and begins the first beat to windward. Many will soon tack on to port in order to find clean air.**

Racing upwind

As well as a good start, to do well on the first leg of a race you have to sail in clear wind. If you are sailing close behind a boat that is to windward or immediately to leeward, it will interfere with your wind and you will not be able to sail fast.

Tack as soon as possible so that you can sail in clean wind. Then, if necessary, tack back again.

'Covering' is a tactic where one boat keeps a rival boat in its wind shadow. Every time the other boat tacks to break cover and find clean wind, the leading boat tacks to re-establish cover and stay ahead.

It's also important to identify and choose the favoured side of the course. Boats can tack up the middle of the course (known as the 'rhumb line'), from side to side all the way across the course, or up one side of the course that may be favoured by better conditions (for instance, more consistent wind, smoother water or more favourable tide). The wind may, of course, change direction. If the wind shifts to the right, the right side of the course will become closer to the windward mark, and vice versa.

Turning round the windward mark

Sound advice is to always make the final approach to a mark on starboard tack. On port tack, you run the risk of being caught by a long line of starboard tack boats. But if you can find a slot to tack round the

Below: **Bearing away round the mark from a beat to a run. The crew is getting the spinnaker pole ready.**

mark, a risky late approach on port tack could be a winning manoeuvre.

Boats tend to bunch up in the final approach to the windward mark, which may create a big problem with turbulent wind. If conditions are crowded, don't attempt to give the windward mark a close shave that requires pointing the boat as high as possible. Delay tacking so that you have sufficient space to leeward to handle the effects of wind shadow. There

Right: **When sailing directly downwind it can be difficult to avoid being 'blanketed' by boats coming up behind. The boat with the blue spinnaker is in danger of being overtaken.**

is nothing worse than hitting or missing the mark, and having to go round it again.

At the top of the course, you will either bear away on to a beam reach or start to head downwind. Keep the boat flat on the water, so that it will bear away easily. Prepare to move weight back as it accelerates on a reach. Don't let the boom hit the mark or you will have to go again!

Racing downwind

If you are racing a dinghy with an asymmetric spinnaker, or any catamaran, it is quickest to reach from gybe to gybe, rather than sailing directly downwind.

However, if you are racing a dinghy with a symmetric spinnaker, or a singlehanded dinghy such as a Laser, it is quickest to sail along the rhumb line directly downwind.

Beware of port-starboard crossings when reaching at high speed under

spinnaker. The starboard tack boat always has right of way – collisions can cause expensive damage.

Boats racing downwind can be affected by wind turbulence. If you are running downwind, a boat directly behind will create a wind shadow and may be able to overtake. If you are reaching across the wind, a boat to windward will create a wind shadow, making it impossible to overtake.

Beware of 'luffing'. It is permitted for a boat to luff above its 'proper course' (directly to the next mark) to prevent a boat to windward from overtaking. It is not permitted to luff beyond head-to-wind. The other boat

must also be given enough time to change its course without a collision. Don't be tempted to get so carried away with luffing that the boats behind can overtake you both.

Approach marks a little wide, so that you're tight beside them after turning the corner, with the daggerboard or centreboard fully down and the sails sheeted right in.

The finish

The race continues to the finish, which may be at the top of the course after another beat, or at the bottom of the course after another downwind leg.

Below: **Sailing home after the race. If you did badly, learn by your mistakes so you can do better next time!**

Optimising the boat

Optimising deck gear and running rigging is an important first step towards slick boat handling and helps to create the perfect sail shapes that are needed for good performance.

Successful racing is about much more than simply generating good boat speed. Every race involves dozens of manoeuvres – tacks, gybes, spinnaker hoists and mark roundings – all of which have the potential to lose valuable time.

Getting the boat set up so that the systems for sail controls fall easily to hand and work perfectly with as little friction as possible is therefore important for your overall performance.

It's also much more fun to sail a boat where all the gear works properly; and it is arguably safer in strong winds, as top-notch sail controls make it easy to flatten sails, and quickly dump power by easing sheets, without excess friction slowing the process. The net effect is that you spend more time sailing and less time capsizing.

Up to standard?

The deck fittings and lines supplied with many dinghies may be substandard for two main reasons. Firstly, to save costs: many manufacturers fit only basic gear as standard, with better quality equipment often available as expensive options. In addition,

the past few years have seen big advances in rope technology and in the deck gear that's used to control all the lines. As a result there are many dinghies – even some that are raced regularly – that will benefit from upgrading deck gear.

Maximising power, minimising friction

The best starting place is often to look at the class association website for your boat – these often detail what is currently considered to be best practice for the boat. The association website should also include a copy of the class rules, which will highlight whether there are restrictions on the modifications

that are permitted – this is often done to ensure boats are equalised and therefore the racing remains close, or to prevent owners with the biggest chequebooks outperforming the rest of the fleet.

If that's not possible, start by looking at each of the systems separately. The mainsheet, for instance, should be easy to pull on hard, even in strong winds, but when the sheet is eased in light airs it should run freely.

Failure to do so may be down to low-grade blocks, in which case they should be replaced with low-friction types. Alternatively, it may be simply that the sheet is too thick to run freely, and if it's replaced with

Below: **Modern quality roller bearing blocks will go a long way to reducing friction.**

> **TIP**
>
> Stretch is bad news for sheets, halyards and other control lines – a very good reason to choose Dyneema over polyester for your boat.

Right: **Control lines leading to each side of the boat enable fine tuning of sail controls without moving crew weight to the middle of the boat.**

a rope of smaller diameter it will work fine.

Ideally the kicking strap, cunningham and mainsail clew outhaul controls should be led to cleats on each side of the boat so that they can be adjusted when both crew are trapezing or hiking hard to keep the boat flat. This generally means that a purchase system is necessary, and low-friction blocks need to be used as the lines will have to turn multiple corners, each of which adds friction to the system.

Below: **If you sail a one-design class, check whether the class rules have any restrictions on changes you're allowed to make to the deck hardware.**

Tuning the rig

Improving boat speed is a combination of honing your sailing skills and making sure that the boat is set up so that it is capable of fulfilling its speed potential.

The starting point is to ensure the rig is correctly tuned. For most dinghies, different settings are needed for different wind strengths, with rig tension increased for strong winds and reduced for light airs. It's also important to get the mast foot (the base of the spar) in exactly the right place so that the rake (fore-and-aft angle) is correct. Not only is this important for speed, but it also has a bearing on the balance of the helm.

If the mast is raked too far aft the boat will tend to turn up too much towards the wind, and vice versa. As well as making the boat more difficult to steer accurately, in both cases you will need more rudder angle to counteract these effects, which will slow the boat.

Tuning guides

The first point of call is normally the appointed (or popular) sailmakers for the class, or the mast manufacturers, as they will both produce tuning guides that detail the recommended settings for various wind strengths. It's also important that your sails are matched to the rig – when a sailmaker produces a dinghy mainsail, the luff is cut to a precise shape that suits the bending characteristics of the boat's mast.

Therefore, for classes that may have a number of different masts, you must find the tuning guide for your rig.

To the outsider it may appear that the small adjustments necessary are barely worthwhile, but the nature of racing is that there's often very little difference between the speed of boats, so every little helps. Even if you don't race seriously, the tuning guide is useful in confirming that your boat is not set up really badly, which would make it less fun to sail.

Friendly help and advice

Don't worry if you find it hard to understand exactly what is needed. If you do, it is worth asking other people in the club or the fleet in which you sail. One of the best things about dinghy racing is that many enthusiastic sailors are willing to share their knowledge to help newcomers. What's in it for them? Quite simply, they understand that the racing for their class – or handicap racing at their club – can only thrive if there's a steady flow of new faces to replace those who inevitably have to leave the scene each year.

Left: **Don't be afraid to ask for help and advice – there are always friendly faces lurking among the sails in the dinghy park.**

Above: **Whatever stage you're at, coaching will improve your skills considerably and help propel you towards the front of the fleet.**

When to invest in sails

As much as boat speed around the racecourse depends on the crew's boat handling abilities, until you reach a good standard in this respect it may not be worth investing in a new suit of sails – the money could be better spent on coaching instead. This approach also has the advantage that the performance gains will stay with you throughout your sailing life, whereas the benefits of new sails start to diminish as soon as they are used.

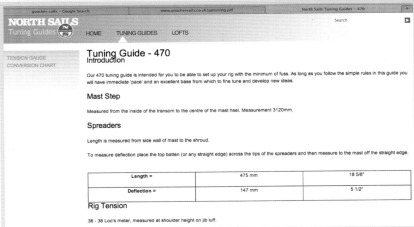

Above: **Most sailmakers produce a tuning guide for each class for which they make sails.**

Winning moves

While slick boat handling and good boat speed are the basic building blocks for racing success, it's also important to make sure you sail in the optimum direction.

The wind direction is never constant for more than a few minutes at a time. This is crucial, especially on the windward legs of the course as tacking on an unfavourable wind shift will give you a big advantage on the new tack compared to boats that stayed on the original one.

Sometimes these changes in wind direction are very subtle, but on other occasions they can be very dramatic. The latter are the ones to focus on first in your racing career – with experience you will become better at identifying the more subtle changes.

Identifying wind shifts

The wind rarely changes strength without also simultaneously changing direction, and generally the bigger the gust the bigger the associated wind shift. Similarly, if you sail into a patch of light wind, this is likely to be blowing from a slightly different direction to the mean wind.

Above: **Dinghies tacking on a wind shift.**

Knowing the rules

Properly understanding the Racing Rules of Sailing (see p110–11) takes time and you're unlikely to encounter every scenario in your first couple of seasons. Too many people, even seasoned racers, fail to keep building their knowledge in this respect, and don't fully understand some of the basics.

Start by looking for changes in the wind strength – often gusts will be associated with a wind shift in one direction, and lulls with a shift in the opposite direction. This knowledge can be used to predict the best times to tack.

It's also important to figure out whether the wind direction is oscillating around more or less the same place, or whether there is a trend towards a permanent shift in the wind direction. The weather forecast – get one that is as detailed as possible – will give you good pointers on this; however, it can only be confirmed for certain by your own observations.

Strategy and tactics

In some situations it will pay to stay towards one side of the course. The best racers will identify a strategy almost instinctively for every race they sail, looking at wind shifts, changes in wind strength across the course, and also the influence of any tidal streams.

Tactics relate to the short-term decisions involving other boats. The biggest single consideration is trying to keep clear of the disturbed air downwind of other competitors. This has to be balanced against also making sure you use the wind shifts to advantage and that you stay on the favoured side of the course.

Above: **If one side of the course is favoured, then the fastest boats will tend to sail on that side, rather than a more even spread of boats across both sides of the direct line between the start line and the windward mark.**

Below: **If you have to fight an unfavourable current or tidal stream, get as close to the shore as safety allows – the stream is always weaker in shallow water and there may even be a favourable eddy.**

Becoming an expert

One of the most compelling aspects of dinghy racing is that there is always something more to learn. When first starting out this may appear daunting, but even those at the top are still pushing boundaries and refining their skills.

Don't worry if initially you're at the back of the fleet – everyone else has been there too, and with a methodical approach a rapid improvement is possible. Developing a mindset that makes analysing and learning from each race an automatic routine is just as appropriate to someone in their first season of racing as it is to aspiring Olympians.

Many clubs and class associations provide excellent coaching sessions, which are usually very effective in helping to take your skills up a level, as well as identifying areas on which to focus afterwards. It also helps to get broad experience, ideally sailing different boats, with different people and in different places.

Seamanship
& cruising

Why cruise a dinghy?

Many newcomers to sailing are pushed into racing almost by default, but don't be discouraged if that's not your thing – there are other ways to enjoy dinghy sailing.

Types of cruising

Dinghy cruising encompasses a wide variety of rewarding activities. One end of the spectrum is gentle, relaxing summer evening pottering or short sails to your favourite waterside restaurants, undertaken only when the weather is perfect.

At the other end of the scale are people who make voyages of up to 12 to 15 hours across big stretches of open water, occasionally even out of sight of land. The ardent enthusiasts also camp on board under a custom-made boom tent. This kind of dinghy cruising can be every bit as skilful and challenging as racing successfully in a world-class fleet.

Shared motivations that drive anyone who cruises or potters in a dinghy include: fun and enjoyment, the sense of being close to nature and the natural elements, and the satisfaction of overcoming challenges. There are also opportunities to visit new places by sea that are seen from a different perspective compared to arriving by land. For many, dinghy cruising is also a family activity with opportunities for shared experiences and learning.

Managing the risks

It's possible to find some organised dinghy cruising – either through clubs, especially those on the coast or large bodies of inland water, and through organisations such as the UK's Dinghy Cruising Association.

Equally, if you're a member of a club that currently only provides racing, you may find a lot of support if you organise a few cruising activities – especially if they are timed at the end of a learn-to-sail course, when there will be enthusiastic people who are looking to take their next steps in sailing.

For many people, however, dinghy cruising necessitates being self-sufficient, including sailing without rescue cover. This has implications for the boat that you choose – you really need to avoid capsizes, so it should have a very stable hull shape. However, it's not possible to entirely eliminate the risk of capsize, therefore the boat also needs to be easy to recover afterwards, without

Below: **Dinghy cruising can be a family activity with opportunities for shared experiences and fun.**

Above: **If sailing for longer distances, the ability to reef under way and understand tides is important.**

being so full of water that it's impossible to sail. Equally, there should be enough buoyancy to support the vessel, plus a healthy reserve, even if it becomes fully swamped with water – see p83.

Gaining the skills

If sailing without rescue cover you need to be a competent sailor who's able to identify risks early enough to take effective action, and be able to interpret weather forecasts effectively. If sailing longer distances, the ability to reef under way is important, as is a solid appreciation of tides and navigation – see p132.

Arguably the skills needed to safely cruise a dinghy cover a broader spectrum than those needed for racing. It would be a

mistake, however, to ignore racing – it's the best way to progress from being an intermediate sailor to an advanced one. Racing can also enable you to push the boundaries of the maximum wind strength in which you're able to sail, in the knowledge that help will be on hand if necessary.

Above: **For many, dinghy sailing is a way of escaping to a relaxing environment, rather than the hustle and adrenaline rush of competition.**

Selecting where to sail

Part of the appeal of cruising in a dinghy is exploring new places.
However, it's important to be able to identify safe places to launch and
to sail and to be able to recognise possible risks.

As your skills improve, you will become better at identifying good places from which to launch and also become more competent at taking difficult conditions in your stride. To start with, however, it is worth choosing locations that are not likely to have many hidden surprises, especially if you have no dedicated rescue cover.

Sheltered water is perhaps the most important consideration – there are many lakes, reservoirs, estuaries and rivers that are suitable, but even a large area of inland water can become challenging if there is a significant change to the weather.

Above all, don't try to emulate the more challenging exploits of experienced dinghy cruising sailors before you have adequate skills.

Coastal dangers

If sailing in coastal areas, it's vitally important to check times of high and low water – many slipways only have access for a few hours each side of high water. Similarly it's important to check tidal streams – these can flow faster than some dinghies are able to sail, which means you may not get back to your launching place. If that stream is sweeping you into open water and out to sea you could get into serious difficulties.

It is also important to be aware of local weather effects, particularly sea breezes (see p148). There are plenty of mornings that start with very light winds, yet by mid afternoon the onshore sea breeze has built to a strength that challenges even experienced dinghy sailors.

Whether on rivers, estuaries or the sea it's also important to be aware of other waterborne traffic, especially large commercial vessels that navigate in narrow, deepwater channels – they may not be able to get out of your way, even in the event of a capsize. The same may

Below: **One of the big appeals of dinghy cruising is exploring picturesque or less accessible places.**

Below: **For your first few outings identify a sheltered area of water, with safe places from which to launch and recover the boat.**

apply to yachts that are in a narrow channel leading to a marina. Study the local charts in advance so that you're aware of all the potential dangers to avoid.

Becoming an expert

Once you have gained more confidence and experience, know that you can comfortably reef under way, and if necessary recover from a capsize in open water without difficulty, you can start to expand your horizons.

While a few brave dinghy sailors have crossed large expanses of water such as the English Channel, this is not to be recommended. However, in suitable settled weather conditions, coastal passages of a few hours'

duration are perfectly possible for well-prepared sailors.

When away for a number of successive days, some sailors also stay overnight on board their dinghy, sleeping underneath a tent over the boom. Larger and stable dinghies will allow you to stay afloat while doing so, without lifting the boat up onto a beach, provided you choose a suitable sheltered location.

Right: **In tidal estuaries and harbours, check the speed of tidal streams. Some can run at 3 knots or more, which can make returning to harbour almost impossible until the stream changes direction.**

Equipment for dinghy cruising

Dinghy cruising inevitably means you'll need to be more self-sufficient than if sailing on well patrolled stretches of water.

In addition to a full set of safety gear – including a handheld, waterproof VHF radio, flares and lifejackets – you will need excellent clothing to keep you warm and dry for extended periods, plus an adequate supply of food and water.

The anchor is an important item of safety gear and should be carried by every dinghy that sails on open water without organised rescue cover. As well as enabling you to stop in a sheltered bay to rest or for lunch, for instance, it's also a safety feature that can be used to prevent the boat being swept out to sea following gear failure.

The anchor needs to be of a size that will hold the boat in strong winds or strong currents – small anchors are likely to be unsuitable for this – and there should be a length of chain of at least 5m (16ft) between the anchor and the warp.

The total length should be at least four or five times the depth of the deepest water in which you may need to anchor. It all needs to be stowed and secured so that it will not fall out if the boat capsizes.

Alternative power

A reliable second form of propulsion is also needed, in case of calm winds and/or in the event of damaged or broken equipment. While a racing dinghy may only carry a single paddle to satisfy this requirement, a cruising dinghy may travel much larger distances. A pair of long oars is considerably better than a paddle

TIP

Always tell someone on shore of your plans for the day, so that they can raise the alarm with the Coastguard if you do not report in at an agreed time.

Below: **Cruising in a dinghy can be a thoroughly rewarding activity, but you need to be able to be self-sufficient if rescue cover is not immediately on hand.**

Far left: **A hand-held GPS chart plotter is really useful.**

Left: **A compass is still an important navigation tool.**

Below: **Paper charts (using waterproof toughened paper) are good for passage planning, as you can spread them out to check potential dangers on route.**

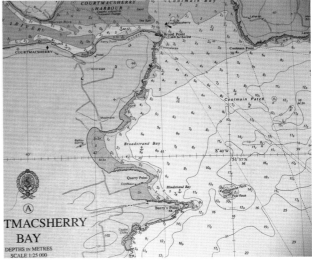

and it's possible for fit and strong crews to row significant distances.

However, even this becomes tiring after a time, so many dinghy cruisers also carry a small outboard motor. It should be stressed, though, that this should be carried in addition to, not as a replacement for, the oars. Finally, a long towline will also help enormously should the boat need to be recovered in bad weather. This should be at least 20m (66ft) long to avoid shock loading – nylon is ideal. On some boats it's possible for the anchor warp to double for this purpose.

Navigation equipment

Charts, tidetables and navigation equipment are also needed for sailing on the sea or in tidal estuaries. Wherever possible, look for charts that are printed on waterproof paper – it's very difficult to keep them dry when sailing in a dinghy. A handheld GPS chart plotter is often a favourite piece of equipment among many dinghy cruisers as it enables navigation to take place while you're under way. However, conventional paper charts should always be taken as a backup – the GPS is not a substitute for a

compass. The most suitable type for dinghy cruising is usually one that allows use as both a steering compass and for taking bearings on other vessels or objects.

Living on board

Enthusiasts who camp on board their boats overnight need a tent over the boom, ideally custom-made to suit the boat, plus camping-style mattresses, sleeping bags and cooking facilities. It's vitally important to keep this kit, as well as your spare clothes, dry. Modern dry bags are extremely effective for this.

Essential seamanship

Don't be lulled into thinking that seamanship is not important on a small boat – it can be argued that the smaller the boat, the more important it is to ensure your safety.

A good appreciation of seamanship is particularly important for anyone undertaking any kind of dinghy cruising, which by its very nature is an adventurous activity. However, seamanship also has an important place in racing – some of the very best racing sailors also have first-rate skills in this respect.

Good seamanship is more than just practising a set of technical skills, it is also an attitude of mind – being aware of the potential risks you face at any particular time and having a strategy to deal with them.

Any environment in which we sail also has the potential to be a very changeable and dynamic one, so it's also vitally important to be aware of any situational changes and to modify either plans or contingencies as necessary.

Sailors who are able to maintain a constant awareness of everything that's happening around them, including other boats (whether dinghies, fishing boats or commercial shipping), changes in the weather and navigational dangers will find that they are rarely caught by surprise. However, it is all too easy to focus so much on the basic mechanics of sailing the boat that you become unaware of almost everything else that is happening around it. Initially it's easy to be a little daunted by this, but don't worry – this is where experience really counts. The more sailing you do, the easier it is to find time to look around outside the boat, and the easier it is to identify the early signs of potential problems.

Below: **Larger boats, whether yachts or commercial shipping, may be very restricted by draught. Make sure you identify the deepwater channels they will use and allow them plenty of space.**

Rowing is a skill that can only be learnt through practice: those who are skilled oarsmen can often propel their boats at a similar speed to those who solely rely on the use of outboard motors.

TIP

It's not paranoid to keep looking around in an attempt to identify potential dangers – the sooner you spot an impending problem, the easier it is to find a solution.

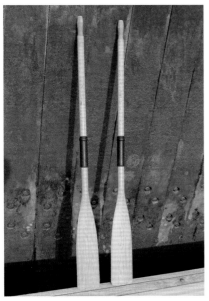

Left: **With practice a pair of long oars provides the most reliable form of alternative propulsion.**

Below: **Good seamanship starts before you even step on the boat – make sure you have an up-to-date weather forecast, the right equipment and knowledge of the local tides.**

Using an outboard

Although convenient in many ways for those who are daysailing or cruising, outboards can also create problems if they are misused. The most important thing is to ensure that the propeller cannot injure anyone – so if there is someone in the water the engine should be turned off, and the kill cord, which is fitted to most engines produced since the mid-1990s, should be worn by the helmsman.

If he/she falls out of the boat this will automatically shut the engine down, eliminating the risk of injuries from the propeller.

While modern engines are generally very reliable they are certainly not infallible and to travel any appreciable distance they use more fuel than many novices allow for. Most small engines of 2hp to 4hp will consume between one and two litres per hour.

It can therefore also be useful to have oars to row the boat home, should the wind become calm.

Tides

If you intend to sail your dinghy in tidal waters, it is important that you have a good understanding and knowledge of the tides and tidal streams.

Tides are caused by the gravitational pull of the moon, and to a lesser extent the sun, on the earth's oceans. This pull creates a bulge in the surface of the oceans in the direction of the moon. Each tidal cycle lasts an average of 12 hours and 20 minutes – so high and low water are separated by just over six hours, although the local geography can affect this.

Spring and neap tides

The position of the moon relative to the sun changes throughout the 28-day lunar month, resulting in the cyclical 'phases' of the moon. When the sun and moon are in line (new moon) or directly opposite (full moon), their gravitational pulls combine to create the largest bulge or 'spring' tides. When they are pulling at right angles to each other (half moon), the forces are decreased, producing a smaller bulge or 'neap' tides.

Spring tides have a high 'high water' and a low 'low water', whereas neap tides have a low 'high water' and a high 'low water'. Spring and neap tides vary cyclically, with the largest springs occurring near the equinoxes.

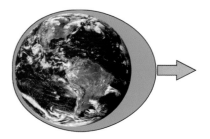

The gravitational pull of the moon on the world's oceans creates a bulge in the direction of the moon, but...

...the solid earth beneath the ocean is also shifted sideways towards the moon, so there's actually a bulge of high water on each side of the globe.

Below: **An understanding of tides is of vital importance for coastal sailing in many areas.**

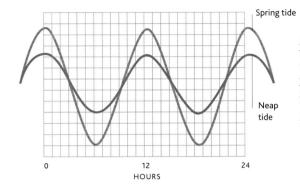

Left: **The difference between spring and neap tides: spring tides have a much larger range between high water and low water than neap tides – high water is higher and low water is lower.**

Tidal data

Tidetables are predictions of the times and heights of both high and low water throughout the year for selected places around the coast. Tidal data can be found in almanacs, on websites or from the local harbour authorities.

Tidal curves are a graphical representation of the variation of tidal height throughout a tidal cycle, which enables us to calculate the height of tide at any given place and time. Increasingly tidal curves can be found online or as smartphone apps, making it easy to look up the predicted height at any given time and location.

Tidal streams

Water tends to flow to the lowest possible level, so it moves 'downhill' from the crest of the tidal bulge towards the trough, creating tidal streams. These tend to run in one direction for around six hours, before reversing and running in the opposite direction for six. The stream is weakest when it changes direction and strongest in the middle of each cycle. The greater tidal range (difference between high and low water heights) of spring tides means the stream flows much faster with spring tides than with neaps.

Tidal atlas chartlets represent the tidal flow at each hour (or half hour) of the cycle with arrows. Alongside the arrows are two numbers which give the speed for spring and neap tides in knots and fractions of a knot respectively.

Tidal curves

These are used to calculate heights of tide at times other than high and low water. Tidal curves are also integrated into smartphone apps that eliminate the manual part of this process:

1. Enter the time of high water, then mark the high water height on the upper scale and low water height on the lower scale. Join the two marks together.

2. To find the height of tide at a selected time, start by entering that time on the grid and draw a line up to the curve.

3. From the intersection of the curve and the vertical line, draw a horizontal line across to meet the angled line drawn previously. Finally draw a line up to the top scale. Find the height of tide above chart datum at this time.

By calculating this you will ensure that you are not left high and dry when you attempt to launch or recover your dinghy after a sail.

Using the tidal curve

HW 1353 UT Ht 4.5m   LW 0656 UT Ht 0.9m   Range = 3.4m

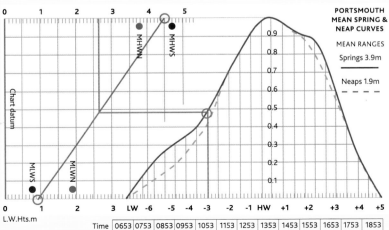

Height of tide three hours before high water = 2.6m

Note that where Daylight Saving Time is practised, you will need to adjust the UT calculations accordingly.

Navigation and chartwork

A basic knowledge of navigation and chartwork is essential for anyone who sails on the sea or in tidal estuaries. Even if you primarily navigate using a GPS chartplotter, navigation at sea is not as straightforward as on land and the consequences of getting lost can be much more severe.

We use cues to navigate when travelling from one place to another. When moving around at home, or driving a car, for instance, we use visual cues to help us recognise where we are and to pick our route.

In nautical terms, this is known as pilotage. If we can see our destination across a lake or bay, for instance, we can just point the boat in that direction, providing there are no dangers in the way and visibility is good. However, if there are dangers nearby we need navigation aids such as buoys – seamarks rather than landmarks. A compass and/or handheld GPS can also be helpful.

Navigation without visual cues
When out of sight of identifiable navigation aids – although not necessarily out of sight of land – navigation traditionally required

positions to be plotted on a paper chart, and a course to steer, allowing for wind and tide, to be calculated. GPS (particularly handheld GPS) chartplotters make this easier, but there are still some fundamental principles to understand.

Compasses and magnetic variation
The Earth's magnetic field is aligned with the North and South magnetic poles, but not with the geographic North and South poles. A compass needle therefore doesn't point towards true north. The difference is magnetic variation, the size of which varies with location around the world, with values mostly between 0–20 degrees.

Charts show magnetic variation at different locations, while GPS units have a database of values, so that the

appropriate correction can be applied automatically, wherever you are in the world. Variation must be applied in the correct direction (either east or west) and you must know whether your GPS is configured to display true or magnetic bearings.

Latitude and longitude
This grid enables specific positions to be easily identified and readily understood by any other vessels. Latitude is measured in degrees north or south of the equator relative to the centre of the Earth. Longitude is measured in degrees east or west of the zero longitude semi-circle – called the Greenwich Meridian – which passes through east London.

Paper charts have a latitude scale each side and a longitude scale along the top and bottom, while electronic charts can be configured so that the

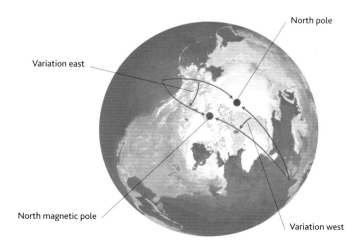

Below: **The difference between magnetic North and true North.**

North pole

Variation east

North magnetic pole

Variation west

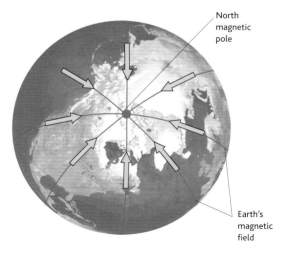

Below: **The compass always points towards the North magnetic pole, unless affected by compass deviation.**

North magnetic pole

Earth's magnetic field

Above: **Paper charts enable you to examine a wide area in detail so are ideal for planning.**

latitude and longitude at the position of the cursor is displayed.

Distance and direction

An understanding of distance and direction is needed for navigation. They can be obtained by measuring between two points on an electronic or paper chart – one nautical mile is defined as one minute (1/60th of a degree) of latitude.

Below: **The latitude and longitude of a position on the Earth's surface.**

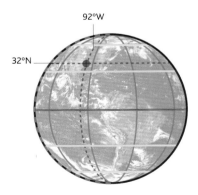

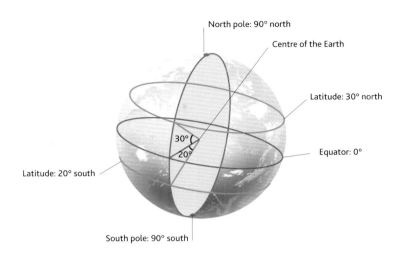

LATITUDE

Above: **Latitude is the angle between a line drawn from any position to the centre of the Earth and the line joining the point on the Earth's surface to the centre of the Earth.**

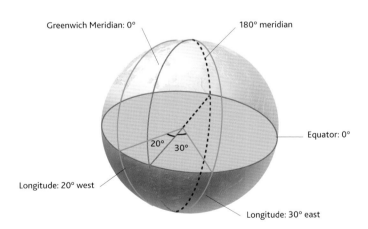

LONGITUDE

Above: **Longitude is the angle between the line joining the Greenwich Meridian and the centre of the Earth and the line joining the point on the Earth's surface and the centre of the Earth.**

Understanding charts

Anyone who sails on coastal waters – whether on the sea or in an estuary – needs to know what hazards and dangers they may encounter, so understanding charts is crucial. The same conventions are used for both electronic and paper charts.

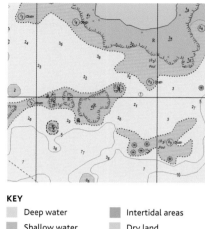

Talking to local sailors will often elicit useful knowledge, but it's also important to obtain and study a detailed chart of the area in which you plan to sail. A handheld GPS chartplotter is also an excellent aid while you're sailing – most are waterproofed to a high standard so you don't need to worry about them getting wet.

However, the small screen of the handheld chartplotter makes it hard to get the overview of an area that you need in order to gain a clear mental picture of the key landmarks and potential dangers. That's why it's also a good idea to have a paper chart that you can spread out and examine closely at the planning stage. This is particularly important if you're intending to sail in unfamiliar waters.

Symbols and scale
While standard international charts use very similar colour schemes and symbols, they are not identical.

Ideally, you should buy a chart symbol guide from the same source as your charts.

Always check the scale of each chart you use – it really helps to have a mental picture of how 'big' a distance of, say, one nautical mile is on the screen or on a paper chart. With electronic charts this will change significantly as you zoom in and out, so it can be easy to lose track of the scale on the display at any given time.

Measuring depths
The level of the sea constantly changes as the tide level rises and falls. Depths of water and drying heights are measured from chart datum, or from the Lowest Astronomical Tide (LAT). This is the lowest level to which the tide is calculated to ever fall due to astronomical influences.

Areas permanently underwater are coloured blue or white – or a mid-blue where it is relatively

KEY

Deep water — Intertidal areas
Shallow water — Dry land

shallow, with the colour lightening as the water deepens. Most charts are now metric publications, with depths shown in metres and tenths of metres.

Areas that are sometimes covered by the tide and at other times uncovered are shown in italics, with the depth underlined. These drying areas are normally coloured green and dry land is yellow.

Underwater dangers such as rocks, wrecks and other obstructions are shown by special symbols, the most common of which need to be committed to memory.

Cross-section of a chart

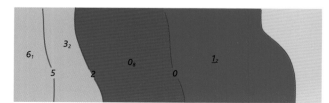

Above: **Depths are marked in metres (and tenths of metres). Underlined numbers show how much they would dry out above chart datum. The depths of water on charts and drying heights are calculated from chart datum.**

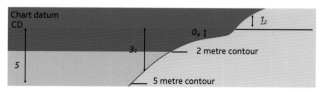

Above: **On British Admiralty charts, depths and drying heights are measured from chart datum, while the heights of objects on land are measured from the level of Mean High Water Springs (MHWS). Some European countries measure the height of objects from Mean Sea Level (MSL), halfway between MHWS and MLWS.**

Position lines

A position line is a line on which your boat is known to be. A transit – when you can see two objects marked on your chart that are in alignment from your position – is the most accurate position line you can get, as you must be somewhere on the projection of that line.

Unless the transit is familiar to you, take its bearing with a compass to ensure you have identified the objects on the chart correctly – this is a common mistake in navigation. Position lines can also be obtained by using a hand-bearing compass to find the bearing of a prominent landmark or other charted object from your boat.

In theory the intersection of two position lines will fix your position, but it's better to use three as this will show any errors. It's rare to get a perfect fix, so the position lines will form a triangle – assume you are at the corner closest to danger.

Below: **A transit – two objects in line such as this buoy and the chimney – makes an accurate and readily visible position line.**

Dangers and obstructions

Certain symbols should be remembered, as you may not have time to look them up before you encounter an unknown danger or obstruction:

Danger	Rock ledge		
Eddies	Wrecks *Depth taken by sounding*		
Overfalls	Wrecks *Showing hull*		
Rock awash	Wrecks *Dangerous*		
Obstruction	Wrecks *Not dangerous*		

If you are approaching a charted symbol you don't recognise, check what it means before you get too close to stop!

How far away are seamarks visible?

Two factors affect the range at which seamarks can be seen. Firstly, the size of most buoys means they are visible only within a range of approximately 2 nautical miles.

Secondly, the curvature of the earth limits the distance to horizon, depending on the height of your eye above sea level. For an eye height above the surface of 2m (6ft 6in) – the maximum realistic height you are likely to achieve in a dinghy – the horizon is a little over 3 nautical miles away.

Passage planning and pilotage

For most dinghy sailors any navigation that's needed consists mostly of pilotage – finding your way around well-marked waters. You won't necessarily need to know where you are at any moment in time, providing you know for certain where any dangers are and that you're well clear of them.

Pilotage is the process of visually positioning the boat using landmarks and seamarks. One of the easiest forms is to follow a narrow buoyed channel – the idea is that boats stay on the starboard side of the channel, although many channels are created for large vessels that need much more depth than a dinghy. The chart and tidal curve or smartphone tidal app will tell you how much safely navigable water there is for your boat outside the channel.

As well as studying local charts, pilot books are useful when sailing in unfamiliar waters. You should also check for local regulations and restrictions – for instance you may be required to keep clear of a deepwater channel. Note that if you launch your dinghy from a beach outside a large harbour, part (or all) of the area in which you sail may be subject to the harbour authority's jurisdiction.

Using a GPS chartplotter

Although a GPS always gives your position, it doesn't tell you how to navigate to a particular location unless you tell it where you want to go by entering a series of positions (waypoints) on your intended route. A waypoint is a geographical position that you want to go to, while a route is a series of waypoints to which you wish to navigate in a specific order.

Once you are under way, the boat symbol on the screen will show the boat's position as it moves across the chart. Usually the screen also shows course over ground (COG), speed over ground (SOG), and distance and bearing to the next waypoint, while a line extended from the front of the boat symbol gives a visual indication of COG. Steer the dinghy so that the boat symbol travels in the correct direction, with the COG line pointing at the next waypoint.

> **TIP**
>
> The COG (course over ground) function of a GPS can be used to help you maintain a direct track towards a destination a few miles away when a tidal stream is setting you sideways.

Using a danger as a waypoint

If the position of a danger is loaded into the GPS, it will display the bearing and distance to the danger, enabling you to keep clear. This can be done by monitoring distance from the waypoint, or by staying on a safe bearing from the waypoint.

In traditional navigation the latter is called a clearing bearing (see bottom right diagram on p139), with a compass used to monitor the bearing from the boat to a seamark or danger you have already identified.

By staying on the deepwater side of this bearing you can be sure you remain in safe water around an unseen obstruction.

Passage planning

Key considerations when planning a passage include the following:

- ✪ The times of any tidal restrictions (tidal heights and strong adverse streams).
- ✪ Dangers that may be encountered, together with strategies for avoiding them.
- ✪ Total distance and estimated duration of the passage given the weather forecast.
- ✪ Alternative plans and destinations in case the weather is not as forecast.

Below: **When sailing longer distances don't trust navigation to luck – make sure you're prepared before leaving.**

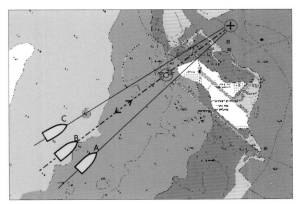

Transit to be followed

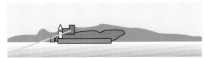

A Right of the transit – turn to port

B On the transit

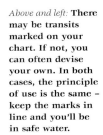

C Left of the transit – turn to starboard

Above and left: **There may be transits marked on your chart. If not, you can often devise your own. In both cases, the principle of use is the same – keep the marks in line and you'll be in safe water.**

Initial transit alignment

The buoy has moved to starboard – turn to starboard

The buoy has moved to port – turn to port

Left: **By sighting a feature like a house in the background and keeping it aligned with the buoy as you approach it, you will ensure that you don't drift down-tide. Remember to alter course as you near the buoy or you will hit it.**

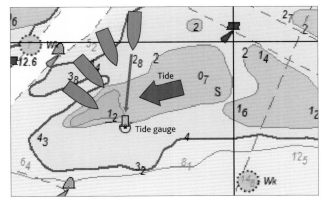

Above: **If you keep pointing the boat at an object, such as a buoy that indicates danger, when there's a cross tide, you stand a good chance of hitting the hazard. As the tide pushes you sideways, with the bows pointing at the buoy, you'll end up approaching the buoy from downtide, which in this case puts you aground!**

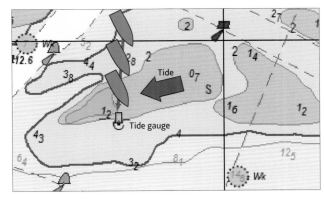

Above: **Make allowance for the tide. This ensures you will approach the buoy on your desired course. You can calculate the course to steer, make an estimate, or stay on the correct COG on your GPS.**

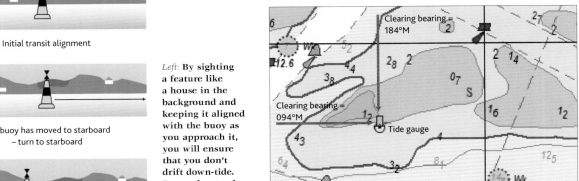

Above: **To avoid the sandbank, use clearing bearings – stay to the east of a bearing of 184°M on the tide gauge and to the south of a bearing of 094°M.**

Weather

Weather forecasts

When sailing we are literally at the mercy of the winds. It is essential therefore to get a suitable weather forecast and understand its implications before going afloat. Wind speed for sailors is generally measured in knots (nautical miles per hour) or as forces on the Beaufort scale.

Sources of forecasts

The internet is an excellent source of weather information, both from national meteorology services such as the UK's Met Office and from third-party providers. If sailing on the sea, look for specialised marine forecasts like the Met Office inshore waters forecast. Don't worry unduly about discrepancies between forecasts that come from different sources – just be prepared for the strongest wind that's predicted from any of them.

In addition, there is an increasing number of locations that relay actual windspeed readings via a website. These can be very helpful in assessing whether the wind is stronger than forecast.

A smartphone enables you to get the latest forecasts before going afloat and there are several useful weather apps – if sailing on the sea, look for specialised marine forecasts.

If you don't have a smartphone, sailing clubs, harbourmasters and marina offices usually display local forecasts, but check you're looking at one that is up to date!

Marine VHF

Coastguards and other authorities broadcast regular weather reports and forecasts on marine VHF radio frequencies. Their websites or sailing almanacs list schedules and relevant channels. In some areas, such as Canada and the USA, these broadcasts are continuous, so you can listen at any time. Coastal and shipping forecasts are also available from both national and local radio. Television can also be a good source of general forecasts, but these are usually tailored to the non-sailor.

Above: **Smart-phones can display weather charts as well as forecasts.**

Above: **A handheld marine VHF radio enables communication directly with the Coastguard, or nearby boats if necessary.**

Right: **This laptop is running chartplotting software on to which wind and weather information can be superimposed, whether it is downloaded from the internet or sent as an email.**

TIP

Listen to what local fishermen or boatmen have to say. Their knowledge and experience of the conditions to be expected can be helpful – but remember that they will be more used to handling strong winds than you are.

Beaufort scale

Forces 0 and 1 (0–3 knots) are so gentle there's not really enough wind to sail.

Force 2 (4–6 knots) is a light breeze and the minimum needed to make progress. Everything will happen slowly so it's ideal for learning.

Force 3 (7–10 knots) is a gentle breeze, when sailing starts to be fun. The boat will start to feel powered up, it will move faster and you will need to use body weight to balance it.

Force 4 (11–16 knots) is a moderate breeze in which wave tops on open water will frequently break. It's a good wind for intermediate and advanced sailors, but difficult for novices without expert help or deeply reefed sails. Dinghies will start to capsize.

Force 5 (17–21 knots) is a fresh breeze with a lot of breaking wave tops. This is getting windy and skilled sailors will love it, but intermediates may struggle and novices will need expert help. Capsizes and breakages become more frequent.

Force 6 (22–26 knots) is a strong breeze and very windy for sailing. It is not suitable for novices, though they may enjoy the experience of sailing in such exciting conditions with an expert on board.

Force 7 (27–33 knots) is a near gale and no longer sailable by dinghies, even on sheltered waters, with the possible exception of those at the very top of the sport.

What causes weather?

Weather has a much more significant effect on activities afloat than on land. The most important ones relate to wind, wave height, visibility and temperature.

Weather is caused by solar heating of the Earth's surface and because the Earth is a sphere, much more solar energy reaches equatorial regions than areas near the North and South poles. The heated regions cause air in contact with the Earth's surface to heat up, reducing its density so that it tends to rise, leading to reduced surface pressure. At the poles, the heavier cold air tends to sink, causing raised surface pressure.

What causes clouds?

Air cools when it rises and its ability to hold moisture decreases. Eventually the air can hold no more 'invisible' moisture, and so cloud forms. Air may rise because it's heated, but also because it's forced to rise by hills, mountains and weather fronts.

What causes wind?

Wind is the result of air moving from high pressure to low pressure. The air rising in the low pressure area needs to be replaced, and this comes from the sinking air in high-pressure regions. The rotation of the Earth causes wind to flow in a spiral pattern, with the wind deflected to the right in the northern hemisphere and to the left in the southern hemisphere as it tries to flow from high to low pressure.

The effect of moisture

There is a large amount of evaporation from the sea, and this moisture is transferred to the air. The higher the temperature, the quicker the evaporation, and unless the air is saturated, with relative humidity of 100 per cent, this moisture will be invisible. Conversely, where the surface is very dry, the air mass will become very dry too.

Types of air mass

A body of air sitting over a continent or ocean takes on the characteristics of that area, being either wet or dry, hot or cold. As it moves away from its source area, it maintains its original characteristics. North-west Europe, for example, encompasses all types of air mass:

Tropical maritime: Air in contact with the warm sea gets warm and moist.

Polar maritime: Air in contact with cold northern seas is cooled – the air is cool and damp.

Arctic maritime: The air is very cold with much reduced ability to pick up and hold water.

Polar continental: The air is very cold from contact with the bitterly cold land and it is also very dry.

Tropical continental: The hot land heats the air, which is very dry.

As an air mass moves, its surface characteristics are modified by the changing character of the Earth's surface. It will be cooled if the surface is cooler; it will become drier if the surface is dry.

Above: **Cells of sinking and rising air cause air to want to flow from high pressure to low pressure. The Earth's spin causes the moving air (wind) to be deflected such that the airflow is not in a direct line from high to low pressure, but starts to form a circular movement instead.**

Seasonal changes

As summer approaches, the rise in temperature lags behind the position of the sun by a couple of weeks over land, but much longer over the sea. Outside the tropics, the sea will still be cool in early summer, but the land heats up and cools down much more rapidly.

The differential between land and sea temperatures has a major effect on weather. The characteristics of the air on either side of the boundary between two adjacent air masses are different. It is these sudden changes that create many of the common weather features experienced in temperate latitudes.

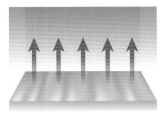

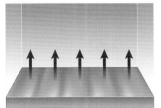

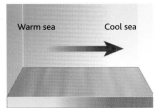

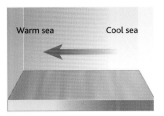

1. Evaporation of water from the warm sea into warm air results in a high moisture content in the air.

2. Evaporation from a cold sea into cold air is much less, so the water content of the air will be less.

3. The air mass is not static. If it moves towards a cooler area, the surface temperature reduces, increasing the relative humidity.

4. If the air mass moves to a warmer area, the air temperature rises. If no more evaporation takes place, the relative humidity falls and the air feels drier.

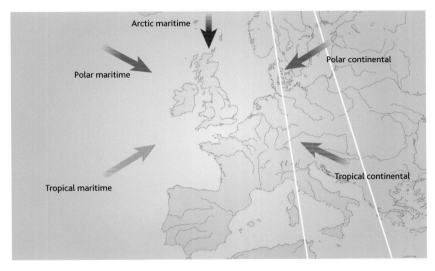

Left: **Air masses take on the characteristics of the 'source' area, which determines initial temperature and water content.**

Below: **Coastal sailors feel the effect of the difference between land and sea temperatures. When a cold airstream travels over warmer sea or land it picks up heat and may form clouds and gusty winds. When a warm airstream travels over colder land or sea it quickly cools and stops rising. This creates a layer of cloud and steadier winds.**

Weather systems

While the accuracy of weather forecasts has improved enormously over the past few decades, it's not always an exact science. Knowledge of the features associated with different weather systems will help you recognise risk factors when the weather deviates from the forecast.

Low-pressure systems

Weather systems are the result of the interaction between areas of high and low pressure. Lines joining places of equal pressure are called isobars. They are just like contours on a map and represent the 'hilliness' of the pressure pattern.

A low-pressure area is like a valley and a high-pressure area is like a mountain. A low-pressure area is one that is low compared with its neighbour, so 1020 millibars (Mb) – now known as hectopascals – is low compared with 1030Mb, but high relative to 1010Mb. Air likes to flow 'downhill' from high pressure to an area of low pressure, but is deflected by the rotation of the Earth to flow almost along the isobars.

Just as the closeness of the contours of a hill show how steep it is, the closeness of the isobars show how steep the pressure gradient is – the steeper the gradient, and the closer the isobars, the stronger the wind.

Two adjacent air masses will have different moisture contents, different temperatures and different stabilities. Even if these differences are small, the two air masses will react with one another. The boundary between different air masses is called a weather front.

Warm front

These are found near the leading edge of a low-pressure system, and are formed by warm air pushing up and over the cold air. They are typically a few hundred miles across, with the uplift of the air causing its temperature to fall and clouds to form.

An approaching frontal system starts at high altitude, with thin, wispy cloud, followed by a steady lowering and thickening of the cloud base. With sufficient moisture in the air, drizzle will start to fall, eventually turning to continuous rain, bringing reduced visibility.

Below: **In a warm front cloud formation is non-turbulent and layered. Water droplets are small and initial rainfall is drizzle. Fog may form where the front is very close to the surface.**

Right: **A cold front is much more active, with a steep frontal surface producing large vertical air currents and towering cloud. Raindrops can be large and hail is possible, as is thunder and lightning. Squally downdrafts of cold air burst from the bottom of the cloud in all directions, with high wind speeds.**

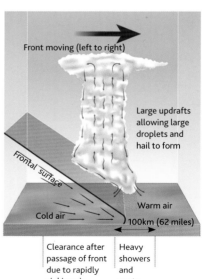

Front moving (left to right)

Large updrafts allowing large droplets and hail to form

Frontal surface

Cold air

Warm air

100km (62 miles)

Clearance after passage of front due to rapidly sinking air – good visibility	Heavy showers and gusty squalls

A COLD FRONT

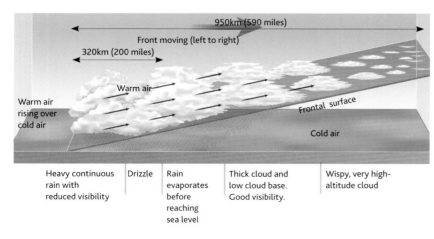

950km (590 miles)

Front moving (left to right)

320km (200 miles)

Warm air

Warm air rising over cold air

Frontal surface

Cold air

Heavy continuous rain with reduced visibility	Drizzle	Rain evaporates before reaching sea level	Thick cloud and low cloud base. Good visibility.	Wispy, very high-altitude cloud

A WARM FRONT

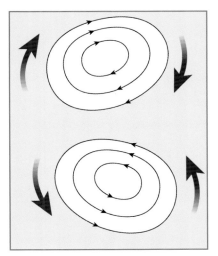

Above: The circulation of air around a weather system in the southern hemisphere is in the opposite direction to the same type of system in the northern hemisphere.

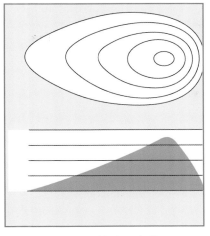

Above: Closely spaced isobars indicate a 'steep slope' producing a strong wind. Widely spaced isobars indicate light winds, as there's not much gradient to drive them.

Above: Where the isobars of a depression are elongated, and turn sharply, cold front-like weather, with heavy rain showers and strong gusty winds, can occur along the trough of low pressure.

As the front passes, the wind direction is likely to shift in a clockwise direction (in the northern hemisphere) while the rain will stop, or at least ease, in the warm sector between the two fronts.

Cold front

The cold front follows the warm front, with cold air undercutting the warm air and causing it to rise. This is a much more vigorous process than in a warm front, but it's also a more distinct feature that's rarely more than 80 to 96km (50 to 60 miles) across.

Cloud forming on a cold front can rise rapidly to great altitudes, producing violent and heavy showers. After the cold front passes, you often get clear skies, with no cloud at all for several hours, but it will feel much cooler in the cold air that follows the front.

Expect squally winds and heavy showers in the immediate vicinity of these clouds, so if possible head to shore or reef your sails early.

Occluded fronts

The cold front will eventually catch up with the warm front to form an occluded front. These are often associated with older and slow-moving depressions. The occlusion may exhibit some of the characteristics of either a warm front or a cold one, with the former often associated with a lengthy period of rain. Low-pressure systems tend to be associated with rapid changes in the weather, so long-range forecasts are likely to be less accurate when high pressure dominates.

Right: Wispy high-level cirrus clouds may herald the end of a period of settled weather in which high pressure was dominant, and signal the approach of a low-pressure system.

High pressure systems

These systems are relatively benign, provided there is not a low-pressure system in close proximity, and they often give long periods of quiet conditions. They are associated with sinking air that warms as it descends, so frequently there's no cloud at all, giving fine, clear weather, although if the air is moist enough, a continuous layer of cloud may form.

Local winds

With local winds, the strength and direction are different from the gradient winds you would expect from examining the isobars. They are temporary, and may be due to topographical features, heating or cooling. In some places they may be so common and pronounced that they have special names, such as the Mistral and the Bora in the Mediterranean.

What is a topographical wind?

Wind is lazy and doesn't like climbing hills, so if a hill gets in the way, the wind will want to flow round it. Because there will be less room for the wind to flow, it will accelerate.

Between islands, there are acceleration zones where the wind may double in strength when it's blowing from certain directions, for example around the Canary Islands. Steep-sided valleys also accelerate the wind in certain wind directions; the Mistral in the South of France is a good example.

Localised heating of the land

In warm, sunny conditions during the summer, the surface of the land heats up rapidly. Air in contact with the land is heated and so rises, causing the pressure to fall, giving a localised low-pressure area. Air rising in these conditions can be quite vigorous. As the heating diminishes, the land cools and the pressure returns to normal.

What is a sea breeze?

If the coastal area is heated during the day, the air rising over it is replaced by air flowing off the sea, the temperature of which has not risen. This is the sea breeze.

The air can rise to a considerable height and require a lot of air to replace it, so the process can be powerful. As the air rises it cools, creating a tell-tale line of cloud just inshore of the coastline. This cool

air is then sucked back out to sea at a height of around 1,000m, before descending again and completing a circulation of airflow.

A clear, calm, sunny morning may well be followed by winds of force 4 or more in the afternoon as the sea breeze sets in.

Keep in mind if you are going to sail in this strong wind that it can extend out to 8km (5 miles) from the coast in good conditions. Then by about 1600 hours the wind will be dropping off, so plan your day accordingly.

Localised cooling of the land

At night, in clear conditions, the land cools, cooling the air in contact with it. The cooled air sinks, giving a localised high-pressure area, which returns to normal once the land is heated again. This is a gentle process.

What is a land breeze?

If the coastal area is cooled during the night, the sinking air will flow out to sea. This is a weak process, so the cooled, sinking air will only flow a short distance, and the resulting wind will be light.

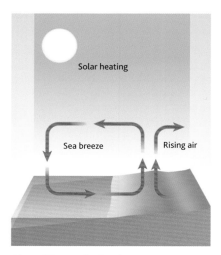

Above: **Where solar heating occurs along the coast, a sea breeze can result.**

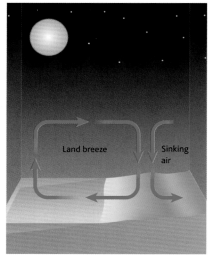

Above: **A land breeze generated by cooling air will be weak, unless the land slopes, in which case it is known as a katabatic wind.**

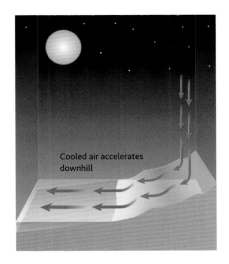

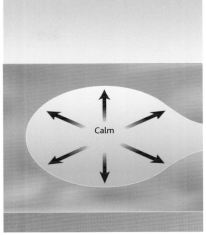

Far left: **A katabatic wind can be quite fierce and the resulting wind flowing offshore can be strong and gusty.**

Left: **A circular sea breeze can be generated over an enclosed body of water.**

What is a katabatic wind?

A katabatic wind is caused by the land cooling, but occurs where the land slopes. The air in contact with the cooled land is heavier and wants to sink. This time it can roll downhill, gaining momentum. The steeper the slope is, the stronger the wind.

Below: **Cumulus cloud forming over the land during the late morning is a clear sign of a building sea breeze, especially if the day started with clear skies.**

On the coast, this fast-moving air can blow out to sea for quite a distance and gale force winds can result where there are coastal mountains. Not only can a katabatic wind be quite strong, it may also be squally. Where a katabatic wind occurs close to a steeply sloping shore, it can literally knock a boat flat, as heeling will not have the usual effect of spilling wind out of the sails.

Local winds on lakes

A sea breeze over a lake or almost land-locked bay can cause a 'circular' wind, where the wind blows on to the shore at right angles all the way round. The wind will be calm in the middle.

Adverse weather

Sudden squalls, fog, strong winds and temperature changes – whether excess cold or too much sun – all have the potential to spoil a day's sailing. However, it's possible to predict the likelihood of these features and make sure you're prepared for them.

The importance of getting a good forecast should therefore never be underestimated – forecast accuracy has improved considerably over the past few decades. However, never assume the weather will stay constant when you're sailing. Although that's often the case, don't risk being caught out by changes in the weather for which you are not prepared.

For instance, if a relatively static area of high pressure is dominating, and the wind is very light in the morning, there's every chance of an afternoon sea breeze (see p148) that could build to a force 5, creating challenging conditions for all but the most experienced dinghy sailors.

Equally, in some parts of the world, such as the Aegean Sea, winds in the morning are frequently calm, but by mid afternoon it may be blowing 25 knots or more.

Strong winds
These are most normally associated with the passage of a low-pressure system, with the wind becoming stronger the closer you are to the centre of the depression. The cold front tends to be the windiest part of the system, so watch out for this when you're sailing (see p147).

Strong winds also form when high- and low-pressure systems are in close proximity to each other, as the isobars are squeezed together. If you're just on the high-pressure side you may experience glorious hot, sunny weather, but with winds approaching gale force. It's easy

Below: **Strong winds require a higher level of skill and physical effort to keep the boat balanced and avoid capsize.**

to be lulled into a false sense of security as the weather seems much nicer than a cold, dull day with less wind, but it would be safer to sail on the dull day.

Sudden squalls

Towards the end of the passage of a low-pressure system, the unstable air at the cold front and in its wake may feature a number of towering shower clouds. These have brief, but intense, periods of heavy rain or hail and strong winds – if you see such clouds approaching it's worth heading for shore before they arrive. If you're too far from shore, then consider dropping the mainsail to depower the boat until the strongest wind has passed.

Temperature changes

New weather features also tend to bring changes in temperature, which can make selecting appropriate clothing a challenge. When on the water it's almost always better to be over-dressed for the conditions than it is to risk getting cold when there's no chance of being able to warm up. If a drop in temperature is expected, dress more warmly than the conditions suggest when you launch. On the other hand if the temperature is expected to rise, don't risk getting cold – it's better to be a little too warm, but make sure you have sun block and plenty of water to stay hydrated.

Fog

This is caused when warm, damp air moves across cold water. Large areas of sea fog are most likely to occur in spring and early summer, when warm, moisture-laden air comes in contact with sea water that has barely warmed up since winter. This kind of fog may last for several days and can be associated with strong winds.

In summer, with high pressure dominating, it's also possible for fog to form on hills at night when the temperature drops rapidly. This then tends to flow down the valleys and out over the coast, but is normally burnt off by the sun during the morning.

Above: **Over a coastline, warm air from the land can react with cooler air over the sea. This cools down the warm air and brings it towards the dew point, where it condenses, creating fog.**

Below: **The black cloud in this squall is a sign of torrential rain, with poor visibility and very strong, gusty winds.**

Choosing
a boat

Analysing your needs

It is so easy to get carried away by the enthusiasm for buying a boat that you can choose one that is totally unsuitable. However, with a little knowledge and a cool head it's possible to find what's right for you.

There's always demand for crews, particularly among dinghy racers, so it's possible to do a lot of sailing without owning a dinghy. Even if your goal is to have your own boat, a short period of crewing for others will enable you to make a much more informed decision about what to choose as your first boat. You will also have access to a network of knowledgeable people whose advice may prove extremely useful.

Singlehanded vs double-handed
Singlehanded sailing is great if you like to sail alone and you never have the hassle of finding a crew. On the other hand, there's no one to confer with or blame if things go wrong! But, singlehanded racing classes are some of the most sociable when you get ashore after sailing.

Double-handed sailing is great for the helmsman, if you want responsibility for how the boat is sailed and where it goes, although at higher levels of competition these tasks are shared more evenly, when the helm is normally responsible for speed and the crew for tactics – identifying the fastest route around the course. Double-handed sailing is also great for the crew on any high-performance boat with a spinnaker, as the crew's role is vital in managing the boat.

Advantages of singlehanded boats
- Singlehanded boats tend to be cheaper than double-handers owing to their smaller size and simpler rig.
- You don't need a crew, so there's no one to organise and you can go sailing whenever you have the time available.
- If you race, you are totally in control of the boat and there's a wide choice of singlehanded classes, many of which get big turnouts at regattas.
- Singlehanders tend to be quick and easy to rig, which minimises downtime, giving you more time sailing and less rigging the boat.

Below: **Singlehanded sailing puts you in absolute charge of the boat, but you will never be lonely in a popular class like the Laser.**

Advantages of double-handed boats

- It's fun to enjoy the sport with a crew and work as a team.
- A double-handed boat can provide more exciting performance, whereas asymmetric spinnakers and a trapeze are only usable on singlehanded boats by experts.
- You can share the time and effort needed to rig, launch and retrieve the boat from the water.
- You may be able to share the cost of owning and running a double-handed boat.

How many crew?

This choice isn't as simple as whether to choose a single- or double-handed boat – some larger dinghies are designed for a crew of three, or with family sailing in mind, although these boats tend to be heavier and less easy to handle on shore. Enthusiastic children are also likely to want to escape to their own dinghies as they get older. All modern dinghies sold in Europe since 1998 are required to display

Left: **Be realistic about your skill level when choosing a boat, otherwise it may prove to be too much of a handful in all but light winds.**

Above: **Sailing two-up on a fast dinghy provides ultimate thrills. Both crew play a vital role – if one makes a mistake, they both take a swim!**

the maximum permitted number and weight of crew.

Weight is also important in that most dinghies are designed with a specific crew weight in mind. If you are significantly heavier than this the boat will be slower and less exciting to sail, while if you are lighter it may be difficult to handle and to keep upright in strong winds.

Skill levels

There's a wide gulf in the ability needed to sail a dinghy intended for novices and a high-performance skiff. Beginners need a fairly stable boat with power and speed that is easy to control. However, with regular practice, tuition and coaching it's possible to progress quickly to a more exciting boat.

Narrowing the field

How do you make the right choice when there are so many different dinghies available? First, decide your priorities so you can then make a shortlist of suitable boats.

Left: **The Topper is a very popular junior racing class that lighter-weight adults can also enjoy.**

Do you want to race?

Dinghy racing is the best way to improve sailing technique. It forces you to make a big effort to learn to manage the boat, and provides a reason to sail on a regular basis. You can meet like-minded people and make new friends by joining a sailing club, which will organise racing over weekends, summer evenings and during special regattas. A major advantage is that a sailing club will also provide safety cover on the water for its members.

Any dinghy can be raced: you just need to find another dinghy to race against. Some dinghies, however, though designed specifically for racing, remain suitable for

recreational fun. These classes have the backing of active class associations, which organise events in many different locations and may also run major regattas such as National or European championships.

Right: **The Xenon combines a sophisticated rig and hull shape with durable moulded construction for low-cost sailing enjoyment.**

Right: **Family sailors need a stable boat with plenty of space.**

Choice of a suitable racing dinghy may depend on local sailing clubs, as many support specific classes to help guarantee good competition. Ideally, each class will race as a one-design fleet of identical boats in which the first to finish wins, but clubs may also organise handicap racing for different types of boat.

One-design dinghies

Most modern dinghies and cats are 'one-designs', with all boats of the class identical, apart from minimal changes to specification.

Many older classes have been updated to keep pace with the times and now allow more modern materials and construction or a more sophisticated modern rig. Therefore a boat designed more than half a century ago (such as the Finn, Optimist or GP14) can be brought up to date and made more rewarding to sail. Dinghies that were constructed originally with marine plywood panels now allow for slight variations in hull shape.

Development class

A development class has few rules, often just maximum length and beam, with no restrictions on sail size or weight. These classes encourage different designs of hull – and are often where innovative ideas are first tried. They tend to be superb but highly specialised racing machines, with a price to match.

Do you want to cruise?

If you have no interest in racing, your first requirement will be a stable boat that handles easily and

performs well. Size will be governed by how many people you want to sail with. A small singlehander may suffice, or you may need a bigger dinghy like a Wayfarer or Topaz Omega, which has room for four people. Many classic dinghies make excellent choices for dinghy cruising. They tend to be more stable than modern racing dinghy designs and are widely available second-hand for those on a tight budget.

Be aware that the bigger the boat you choose the heavier and more difficult it will be to handle on dry land. Pulling a dinghy back up the slipway is a necessary part of sailing, but make sure it doesn't ruin your enjoyment of the sport!

It may also be worth considering a crossover boat. This is one that combines the ease of handling and excitement of a dinghy with some of the advantages of a larger boat, such as a small cuddy that has potential to provide shelter, or a lightly ballasted (weighted) lifting keel that will help to provide stability and resistance to capsize.

Types of construction

When choosing a dinghy, it's important to understand the different types of construction and materials used. This will not only help you select a boat that meets your needs, it will also give you a head start in the knowledge needed to go after it properly.

Glassfibre

This is the material from which most dinghies are built – it's a well-proven and inexpensive way of producing relatively light yet long-lasting boats in both low and high volumes. Provided it's not abused, the structure has a very long potential life, and many repairs are within the scope of amateurs.

Solid glassfibre construction, however, has to some extent lost favour among the most competitive racers. Where class rules allow, they tend to favour a sandwich construction, usually with foam bonded between two thin layers of glassfibre, and often employing epoxy resin in preference to the standard polyester resin. This provides a stiffer structure that does not flex under the considerable loads imposed by the rig in strong winds, with the result that for a relatively small increase in building cost the boat retains a much longer competitive life.

Rotomoulding

This is a more expensive form of boatbuilding, but produces extremely strong and almost indestructible craft at a low unit cost. On the downside, rotomoulded boats are heavier than glassfibre equivalents, and in the unlikely event of the structure being damaged are more difficult to repair. Rotomoulding is generally used for training and family boats, where ultimate performance is not a key criterion, but a strong boat at a good price is an important consideration.

Plywood

Many dinghies were built from plywood, often by their owners, when dinghy sailing became popular during the 1950s, 1960s and 1970s. Advantages are that it is a relatively cheap, yet stiff and strong material

Right: **Sophisticated epoxy foam sandwich construction ensures that this skiff is light and stiff. This type of construction can provide top performance for many years.**

Below: **Glassfibre is a strong and relatively inexpensive material for dinghy construction.**

Above: **Rotomoulded dinghies are extremely tough and almost maintenance-free, but you still need to beware of scratches!**

Right: **This all-wood singlehander is a beautiful boat, but will require extra time, maintenance and money to keep it in tip-top condition.**

from which a lightweight boat can be built; however, it's much more labour-intensive than more modern construction methods, and even the best marine-grade plywood is susceptible to rot and delamination. Despite these drawbacks the material was used for many of the best racing dinghies until epoxy and foam sandwich became widespread.

Planked timber

Traditional carvel- or clinker-planked dinghies were the norm until plywood construction took over, and are still held in high regard by enthusiasts. They can look great, and some second-hand examples are available at a good price, but repairs can be expensive and time consuming, and new boats are often eye-wateringly expensive.

Carbon-fibre

This is the preserve of very high-end racing dinghies, where maximising strength and minimising weight are the overriding priorities, irrespective of cost. It is a state-of-the-art material, and it is impossible not to admire the technology in the best boats, even if you don't aspire to own one yourself.

Buying a second-hand boat

Sailing dinghies have an intrinsically long lifespan – several decades is the norm – which means most sailors have boats that they bought second-hand. When buying a second-hand boat, however, it's important to recognise that the replacement value of sails, deck gear, trailer and other equipment may exceed the overall value of the boat, especially on

older craft. It's important therefore that these are in a good serviceable condition – if not, the hull and rig of an older or unpopular boat may have little or no intrinsic value.

Of course the structure of the boat should also be in good order – if there's evidence the boat has not been taken care of you should look elsewhere. This is particularly important with wooden dinghies, which need a lot of regular maintenance to keep them in good order. Pay particular attention to the mast base, centreboard or daggerboard case, rudder pintles and buoyancy tanks.

Why choose a catamaran?

Basically, catamarans are faster than dinghies. Two slim hulls are easier to drive through the water than one wide hull. Connected by two aluminium beams, they form a wide 'platform' for the crew, which helps provide sufficient leverage to hold down a big and powerful rig – particularly if the crew hang out on trapezes.

What are catamarans made of?

Most racing catamarans will have glassfibre foam sandwich hulls, which provide the best compromise of stiffness and weight.

Each hull is built in two-part moulds that allow bulkheads to be incorporated. This creates a light, stiff structure combined with the foam core, with the two halves of the hull mould bonded together and ready for fittings to be attached. Rotomoulded polyethylene is used to build durable cat hulls at the lowest possible cost. Popular models include the Dart 16, Hobie Twixxy and Topaz 16CX.

How much wind?

The amount of wind required to start sailing will depend on a mixture of factors:

- ✪ Sail power, determined by area, height and efficiency of the rig.
- ✪ Width and weight of the catamaran's platform.
- ✪ Weight and leverage of the crew.

Most cats need force 3 to start sailing fast, will be at full potential speed in force 4, and will be maxed out in force 5, at which point crew skill and ability to depower the rig becomes essential.

The most stable sailing platform

One good reason for choosing a cat is that the crew's 'platform' provides a much more stable base than any dinghy when sailing at speed. This makes cats ideal for learning and experiencing the delights of the trapeze, which is both more efficient and more pleasant than hiking over the side.

A cat also provides a great way of learning to handle an asymmetric spinnaker, with the mouth of its chute projecting in front of the boat where it is clear of the forestay and bridle. This ensures the spinnaker hoists and drops will not snag.

The stable cat platform is a huge bonus when the crew is gybing the spinnaker or trimming the sheet out on the trapeze wire, plus there is the

Right: **Wow! This looks difficult, but it's actually very stable and easy to sail a cat like this Hobie 15 at 45 degrees. However it's not a good way to sail fast!**

> **TIP**
>
> Cats are best in wide open areas of water, so make sure you have enough space. Some sailing clubs encourage cats; others think they sail too fast or take up too much space.

Above: **Many recreational cats have shallow skegs on each hull which are sufficient to prevent side-slip, but many racing cats have removable daggerboards for extra lift.**

Above: **The Topaz 14 Xtreme combines low-cost rotomoulded hulls with a high-aspect rig, providing lots of power for one sailor on the trapeze.**

major advantage that the spinnaker provides lift, which helps prevent the leeward bow from nosediving.

Curiously, the spinnaker doesn't make a big difference to the cat's speed through the water downwind, and probably makes it slower upwind, due to the extra weight and clutter. However, a spinnaker provides the power for a cat to bear away on the apparent wind and sail deeper downwind than with two sails, reducing the distance it has to cover. The bottom line is that trapezing and spinnaker sailing provide loads of extra fun for cat sailors!

What else do you need?

As well as buying the boat you also need to set some of your initial budget aside to pay for all the essential accessories. These will vary to some extent depending on your intended use of the boat, but will always need to include a launching trolley and a cover.

Trolley

All dinghies require a launching trolley to push the dinghy to and from the water. The trolley should have a galvanised steel frame with a shaped support for the hull and inflatable tyres to make it easy to pull or push. If you launch over a sandy beach or shingle, larger tyres will be helpful.

Trailer or trailer-trolley

To transport a dinghy by road, a trailer with a heavy-duty galvanised steel frame and mast support, roadworthy wheels and tyres, and supports for the hull, is essential.

You will also need a trailer-board for the number plate with brake, indicator and reversing lights, plus straps to hold the boat down. The car must be fitted with a suitable towing ball and socket for the trailer lights.

Always launch and retrieve a dinghy on its trolley – if the trailer wheels are immersed in water the wheel bearings will be progressively damaged and may seize, particularly if they have been exposed to salt water. Purpose-built combination trailer-trolleys are therefore the perfect solution. The trolley slides on and off the trailer on rollers and is secured to the trailer at the front. The trolley always supports the boat.

Different countries have different towing regulations and maximum permitted speeds.

Covers

For protection in the boat park, a dinghy needs a waterproof top cover which may be available in boom-up or boom-down design. A bottom cover will protect the hull from road dirt and stone chips when trailing.

Foils on high-performance dinghies tend to have fragile tips and edges. They should be stored and protected in padded bags designed

Below: **The launching trolley should support the hull, with guides to hold it in place when the boat is semi-afloat. Most modern trailers are part of a combi-trailer system – this means the boat and its trolley can be pulled directly onto the trailer.**

Above: **When trailing, the boat is protected by top and bottom covers. A trailer board with number plate, brake and reversing lights, and indicators is a legal requirement if you trail on the road. Effective straps are vital to ensure the boat is securely held on to its trailer.**

for the rudder and daggerboard. Carbon masts will slowly deteriorate when exposed to UV light so a mast sock cover is recommended.

Insurance

Third-party insurance is mandatory at most sailing events and is strongly recommended for all dinghy sailing. Comprehensive insurance against theft, loss or damage is likely to be worth the additional premium as boat repairs and replacement can be very pricey.

Optional extras

If you buy a new dinghy, a wide range of optional extras may be on offer: a different coloured hull and waterline, padded foot straps, top-rated blocks and control gear, additional control systems, high-performance foils (these are stiffer and lighter), carbon spars (in place of aluminium), and carbon reinforcement in the hull.

Accessories

- A wind indicator, such as the highly responsive Windex, is invaluable for showing the exact direction of the wind. It can be mounted on the bows or front of the mast on a singlehanded dinghy with just a mainsail, or on the top of the mast when the dinghy has a jib.
- As well as telling the time, a waterproof sailing watch provides a vital countdown facility if you go racing.
- A compass attached to the deck or mast allows you to spot wind shifts and may be required to plot a course. Conventional and digital dinghy sailing compasses are available.
- A GPS will settle all questions on how fast you can sail and can also be used for long-distance dinghy cruising or racing. A small, waterproof GPS unit can be worn on your wrist, stored inside your buoyancy aid pocket or be attached to the mast at deck level.
- It is advisable to carry a purpose-designed safety knife when you go sailing. This can easily be carried in the pocket of a buoyancy aid. A stainless steel multi-tool is invaluable when rigging or packing a dinghy onto a trailer. At the very least you will need some kind of tool for undoing stiff shackles.

WIND INDICATOR

WATCH

COMPASS

GPS

SAILING KNIFE

Looking after
your boat

Dinghy care

Look after your boat and it will look after you; neglect it though and it will get shabby, lose its value and be less reliable.

No salt!

If you have been sailing on the sea, always wash off the salt afterwards – it corrodes fittings, abrades sailcloth and speeds the deterioration of your boat. Use a hose to wash everything, and then leave the boat and its sails to air-dry, but do not let them 'flog' or flap in the wind to dry.

Clothing care

Dunk your wetsuit, boots, buoyancy aid and anything else in fresh water to get rid of any salt. Otherwise it won't dry properly, zips will corrode and seize up, everything will feel sticky and the colours will fade.

Below: **A Dacron sail can be rolled or folded, but avoid hard creases. A Mylar laminate sail should only be rolled. If it is creased, it will crack.**

Hang your wetsuit or drysuit on a hanger in a cool, dark cupboard. Check drysuit seals and replace any that look ready to tear. Wax the heavy-duty drysuit zip to ensure it will open and close easily.

Neoprene boots can get smelly, generally caused by wearing them on a hot day. Water won't wash the smell away. Use a nappy-washing solution to kill the bacteria inside.

Boat cleaning

If a hose is unavailable, a sponge or wet cloth and a bucket of water should be sufficient to properly clean the hull and deck. Acetone, carefully applied and wiped on with a rag, will remove deeper grime. Avoid domestic cleaning products, which may leave a slippery residue. Specialist boat cleaners include non-slip polish.

Sail care

Wash dirty sails with warm water and detergent, then rinse with cold, fresh water. Do not attack sails with a hard-bristle brush, or use chemicals or bleach.

Allowing a sail to flap in the wind to dry (flogging), prematurely ages all types of sailcloth, so should be avoided. Sails also deteriorate in strong sunlight so store them out of the light. If you leave the dinghy in a boat park with the jib rolled, use a protective zip-up sock to cover the sail. Roll laminate sails from head to foot parallel with the battens. Dacron sails can be rolled in a similar fashion, or flaked in a series of folds. Take out the battens or release batten tension.

Avoid storing a sail that is still wet. Spinnaker cloth is particularly susceptible to mildew, which is difficult to remove.

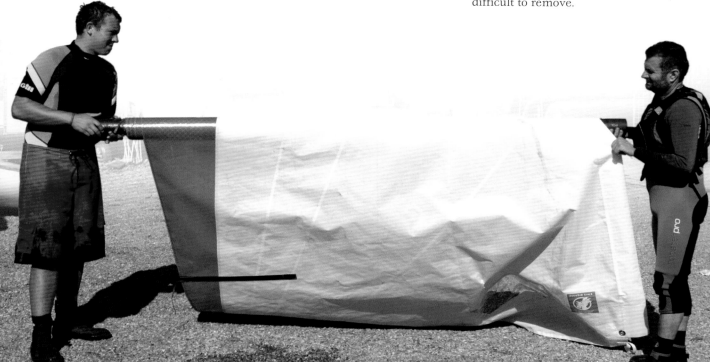

Left: **Find a clean space to work on your boat and make sure everything is packed so it will be in top condition next time you go sailing. Beware of tar on the beach or dirt on the grass!**

For extra safety, consider lowering the mast. Be aware of your next-door neighbour though!

Home storage

Make sure the boat is well supported so it cannot sag – this is especially important for wooden, polypropylene or polyethylene hulls, which can deform relatively easily. Support the mast so that it is absolutely straight.

Left: **Protect your gear. A padded bag protects the rudder or daggerboard foils and a long, tubular bag pads the mast.**

Below: **When towing on the road, use top and bottom covers to protect the hull.**

Boat park storage

Drain all water out of the boat. Unscrew inspection hatches and dry the inside of the hull with a sponge. Remove the drainage plugs to allow air to circulate inside the hull. Just remember to put them back in next time you go sailing!

Secure the cover with all the straps pulled tight under the hull. Make sure water cannot leak inside. If you have a boom-up cover, there is often a problem with rain getting in by the mast. Leave the dinghy bows-up, or with self-bailers open, so that water can drain straight out.

Make sure the dinghy is securely attached to ground anchors as dinghies that blow over in storms can cause carnage in the boat park.

Dinghy care (2)

Make regular checks to keep all your dinghy equipment in tiptop condition. It will reward you with safer, less expensive sailing throughout the season and you will be able to pre-empt many breakages.

Left: **Look at all that string! This racing dinghy has complex rig controls – a lot to replace when it wears out.**

What needs checking?
- Check the boat after each day afloat and replace anything that's not in perfect order.
- Sheets and control lines fray if the same area is regularly gripped by a ratchet block or rubs against a fairlead. The frayed area will slow the rope down as you ease or tension it, and may also break. Replace it as soon as possible.
- Shock-cord is used to keep many items under tension, including trapeze wires, toe straps or the continuous halyard/retrieval line for the spinnaker, and to hold the rudder or daggerboard down. Shock-cord should be replaced when it becomes permanently stretched and loses its recoil.

- Spring-loaded cleats will lose their spring eventually. Wash out salt to prevent corrosion and give them a spray with silicone. If a spring wears out, the whole cleat will need to be replaced.
- Shrouds are strong, but individual strands of the wire can break – a particular problem with roller-furling forestays. The top swivel often doesn't turn as freely as the bottom one, straining individual strands and eventually breaking them. Replace the shroud or risk the mast falling down.
- Check for corrosion or weakness where the shrouds and forestay are attached to the mast. Then check the chain plates and forestay connection at the bow.

Foil dings
- Centreboards, daggerboards and rudder blades are prone to 'dings' caused by hitting the bottom. The more fragile the foil, the worse the ding will be. You can ram a moulded plastic foil into the ground and only get a few scratches, but the same impact will knock the bottom off a lightweight laminate foil.
- Do not ignore damage; it will only get worse. Minor dings can be repaired with gel coat filler rubbed back to a smooth finish with wet and dry sandpaper. If a bigger chunk has been knocked off the foil, build up the area with marine epoxy filler, then sand it to the correct shape.

Right: **A glass-sheathed, laminate wood foil requires careful handling. If you let it hit the bottom, the leading edge will get damaged.**

Far right: **Boat fittings will loosen with extended use. Check the rudder is a tight fit inside its stock and that the pintles are secure in the transom.**

Rope and canvas care

The specialised lines used on performance dinghies can be expensive to replace, so it's worth looking after them. Rope ends need protection against fraying. Most new lines have ends sealed with a hot knife, but a sailmaker's whipping, stitched through the rope, is the best permanent solution.

Chafe can rapidly weaken a rope, so it is important to ensure lines are led clear of anything that may rub and cause damage. Small amounts of chafe won't seriously weaken a line, provided the affected area isn't exposed to further damage. The lifespan of many lines can be extended by 'end for ending' them – reeving them the opposite way round, so that any further chafe occurs on undamaged parts of the rope.

Covers also need to be looked after to maximise their lifespan. Check stitching regularly, especially in the high-load areas around the tie-down points, and repair any damage immediately.

Rips and tears should have frayed edges cut away with sharp scissors, and a neat hem sewn around the damage. A slightly larger patch can then be stitched around the damage.

Mould and algae grow on damp fabrics, or where dirt accumulates. Regularly washing salt and dirt away with fresh water helps the fabric dry quickly, as does reproofing with a spray-on reproofing liquid.

Hull dings

✪ Polyethylene and polypropylene hulls are not suitable for amateur repair, so it is just as well they are bash-proof, although the plastic can scratch badly. These scratches are rarely serious, unless you're racing at a very competitive level, when they will have a marginal effect on performance.

✪ Glassfibre is more susceptible to minor impact damage, but is reasonably easy to repair. Glassfibre repair materials should only be used in dry, dust-free conditions with a reasonably warm temperature.

✪ Damage to the outer skin of the gel coat can be repaired with a correctly colour-matched, two-part gel coat. Sand the damaged area until it is smooth before applying the gel coat.

✪ More extensive damage, which may require cutting through the glassfibre into the foam core, is best handled by professionals, as it's important to get everything absolutely right.

GRP dinghy repairs

Dinghies are normally lightly constructed out of glassfibre (known as GRP), yet they are often subjected to harsher treatment than larger boats. This is particularly true for dinghies that are dragged up stony beaches, or for those that sustain damage when tied alongside a quay.

Above **It's important that the structure of your dinghy is maintained in good condition for both optimum performance and safety.**

Below **Dinghies tend to be lightly built, so damage that might be cosmetic on larger boats may turn out to be more serious.**

Rubbing strakes, whether timber or rubber, are often one of the first components to show wear. The most common problem with the rubber types that wrap around both sides of the gunwale is that they pull through their fastenings. Refitting these with larger washers will often give the rubbing strake a new lease of life.

Rubber types that slot into an aluminium backing can be more difficult to deal with if the rubber pops out of place. Patience will often pay dividends here – in winter, heat the rubber carefully with a hairdryer to make it softer and more malleable. A few blobs of adhesive will help keep it in situ.

Wooden rubbing strakes rarely sustain damage along their entire length, so a graving piece or short length can be scarphed in to replace a damaged section.

Bilge runners

These can be vulnerable to significant wear, especially on tenders that are frequently beached, or dragged into the water from a concrete slipway. Plastic or brass rubbing strips can protect the bilge runners to a certain extent, although the screw holes may allow water ingress into the hull.

With moulded glassfibre bilge runners, start the repair by cutting away any damaged material. Thoroughly dry the hull, before

filling any voids and screw holes with a mix of resin and colloidal silica or microfibres. Additional layers of glassfibre can then be laminated on top of the runners to restore them to the original strength specification.

A dinghy can be repaired easily, possibly without too much attention to achieving a perfect cosmetic finish. However, it's a different matter for a specialist racing dinghy, where a good fairing job will be needed to make a perfect finish.

Above **Dinghies with a double hull can be unsafe if a layer is damaged, as the void between the two skins can fill with water.**

Small glassfibre repairs

At first sight this looks like only relatively light damage...

...but once the loose material is removed the problem extends further.

The hole, with all unsound material removed and ready for laminating.

With three layers of glassfibre mat in place, it's ready for final finishing.

Double-skin dinghies

Many dinghies and other small boats are built by joining two glassfibre mouldings together, with the void in between filled with foam. When these boats are new, they have the advantage of ample built-in buoyancy. However, if either of the two skins is punctured – or the join between them is damaged – water can flood between the two compartments.

A major problem with this is that there's no way of measuring how much water has got in.

Most frequently, the problem is that the joint between the two mouldings has been damaged. The best solution is to separate them, remove the foam, repair any other damage, and then rejoin the two sections, ensuring the joint is completely waterproof. This can be achieved by bedding them together on an adhesive filler, made by mixing epoxy resin and microfibres. Laminating two layers of glassfibre over the join will then ensure it remains watertight.

GRP hull repairs

A large hole in a glassfibre dinghy can be awkward to repair, especially if it's on a corner, a chine, or through a part of the hull made inaccessible by a watertight chamber. However, it's almost always possible to find a solution to any type of damage.

When a dinghy is damaged in the lower part of the transom, there is likely to be a watertight buoyancy chamber on the inside which will make access difficult or impossible. The trick is to make a former, which can be inserted through the hole and then bonded to the inside of the hull. This makes a 'wall' which can support the lay up.

The first task is to clean up the edges, and then grind them back with a coarse grit (P60) disc on an angle grinder to make a shallow 2in (5cm) feathered depression all round.

The opposite corner of the boat is used as a mould. Clean the hull, allow to dry, and then apply three layers of release wax. Lay some

6oz (150g) woven GRP cloth over the corner and thoroughly wet out (ie saturate) with epoxy, forcing it down with a roller until it has taken the shape of the underlying hull.

Next, cover it with peel ply. This is a layer of woven Dacron cloth that's removed once the epoxy has cured, leaving a surface that's ready for bonding in the next stage.

Lift off the mould, and transfer it to the opposite side, orientating it to fit. You will be able to see the hole through the material, so now draw

the outline of the extremity of the feathering. Cut around this outer line with a bandsaw or scissors. The resulting cut-out will form a backing plate, which will be flexible enough to insert through the hole. Roughen the insides of the hull around the hole as well as you can with coarse sandpaper prior to fitting.

Drill a small hole in the middle of the cut-out, and fit a screw to act as a handle. Liberally coat the edges of the cut-out with a quick-drying epoxy where it will meet the hull,

Below **Tight racing in a close fleet is great fun and while sailing is a non-contact sport, bumps and knocks do occasionally happen in these situations.**

Right **The buoyancy tanks inside this dinghy make this a tricky repair. Here, the edges of the hole have been trimmed and feathered to create a depression.**

and then push it through the hole. Using the screw, pull the cut-out firmly back so the glue can make contact, and hold it until the glue has hardened.

Place a clear polythene sheet over the reinforced hole, and draw

Patching a hole

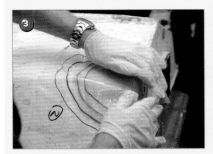

To create a backing pad, apply three coats of release wax to the undamaged corner. Wet out some woven roving, cover with peel ply, and allow to cure.

Remove and trim the backing pad. Apply quick-drying epoxy to the edges, insert it into the hole, and use a screw to pull it up tight.

Use a clear sheet of polythene as a guide for the repair patches. Wet them out together, with the largest diameter pad at the bottom.

Remove the polythene, apply the patches, and smooth with a brush. Once cured, apply epoxy filler to fair the hull prior to sanding and painting.

a series of rings to represent the ½in (12mm) contours of the feathered depression. These contours will be used to shape a series of reinforcement patches. Cut out the patches according to the contours, and then lay them on the polythene, starting with the smallest one and progressively getting bigger so the largest is at the top.

Pour activated epoxy (ie mixed thoroughly with hardener) onto this patch sandwich, and gently work over it with a spatula until all the patches are thoroughly wetted out. Pick up the polythene from underneath, and then lay it over the hole so the patches come into contact with the feathered depression. Use the contours as a guide. You want the widest patch to meet the hull first, with the increasingly smaller ones making the lay-up thicker towards the centre and forming a plug.

Peel away the polythene. The resulting lay-up may be a little distorted, so work it over with a brush or roller until it is as smooth as possible. A final decorative touch is to sand the entire hull and give it a coat of two-pack paint. If faired and painted properly, the repair will be invisible.

Repairing foils

A smooth flow of water over rudders, centreboards and daggerboards is vital for a dinghy to handle as it was designed, and for top racing performance. However, these items are easily damaged, especially on their fine trailing edges or along the lower edge, as a result of grounding.

Checking structure

Most older dinghies have foils that are made of marine plywood, although newer boats tend to use glassfibre instead, often with epoxy reinforcements. The reinforcements may also incorporate a foam or honeycomb core to create a stiff but lightweight structure.

Before undertaking repairs, it's important to assess whether the foil still has adequate structural strength. Centreboards and daggerboards are most prone to failure at the point where the foil exits the hull when in the fully lowered position. This is the first place to look for evidence of stress cracks. In a glassfibre structure, these should be ground out; if they penetrate no more than 10–15 per cent of the foil's thickness, the material removed can be made good with new glassfibre. Deeper cracks almost always mean structural strength has been compromised and the foil needs to be replaced.

Checking the core

You also need to check the glassfibre skin to see if water has reached the core, as this can dangerously compromise strength and stiffness. Inspect any damage and poke it with a small screwdriver. If this sinks deep into the foil, then water is certain to have reached the core.

However, if the surface can't be punctured, the core is probably dry. The same principles apply for rudders, although the most usual point of failure for the blade is at the bottom of the stock.

Repairing edges

Start by carefully removing any loose or cracked material with a sharp chisel, then thoroughly clean and de-grease the surfaces. A filler made of epoxy resin thickened with micro-balloons can be used to repair small chips and nicks, although a 50:50 mix of micro-balloons and microfibres (which add some structural strength and are sold as fillers) is better for larger areas of damage.

Left: **The dings in the edges of this Laser daggerboard will impair its performance and handling, but are easy to fix.**

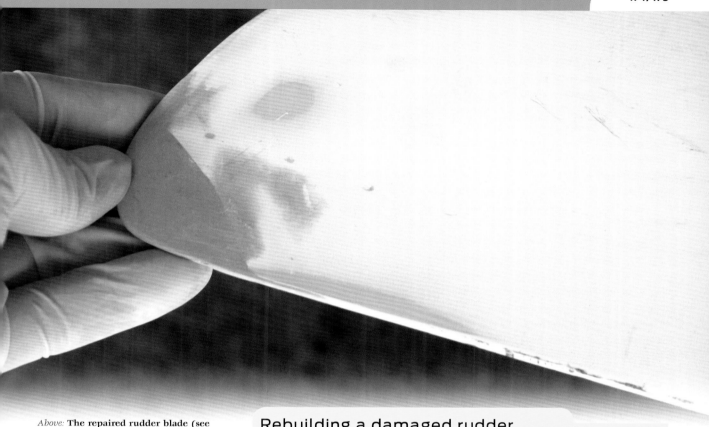

Above: **The repaired rudder blade (see right) after fairing to shape. It is now ready for repainting.**

The trailing edges of foils are often very fine and fragile, so large areas of damage – over about 2.5cm (1in) in the fore-and-aft direction – will benefit from additional support. Inserting stainless steel pins into the after edge of the sound material will solve this problem.

The final part of the task is sanding the repaired foil to fair it to the original shape. This requires both patience and a fine eye, but spraying the area with a high-build primer will help to show imperfections clearly, while filling some of the hollows. To get a perfect shape may require a few cycles of filling or priming, then sanding. The foil can then be painted to achieve a good final finish.

Rebuilding a damaged rudder

Start by inserting stainless steel pins to give the repair structural support.

Tape a temporary support on the underside to prevent the filler sagging.

Apply the epoxy filler. Two or three applications are needed on each side.

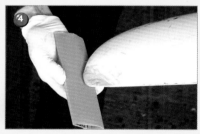

Sand the repair back to a fair finish that blends in with the rest of the rudder.

Buoyancy tank leaks

Dinghies are prone to capsizing and swamping, and so must have sufficient buoyancy to support their own weight, plus that of an outboard motor, anchor, and any other gear carried. However, this safety feature can easily become compromised.

Testing buoyancy tanks at least once a season is the only way to be sure of their continued integrity. There are two approaches to doing this: submerging the boat for 30 minutes, or lightly pressurising the tanks with air and checking the pressure is maintained for at least ten minutes. The former has the advantage that any leaks will be immediately obvious thanks to the stream of bubbles that will stem from the smallest of deficiencies.

However, it may not always be easy to do this, especially if working on the boat at home, as dinghies are not designed to support the weight of a full load of water inside when onshore. This is particularly true of lightweight racing dinghies.

The alternative is to lightly pressurise the tanks with air from a foot pump – many inflatable dinghy pumps will fit the bung (drain) holes at the bottom of the tank. Leaks can be found by putting a detergent solution around the edges of the tanks and any fittings, including inspection hatch covers.

In most cases, it is these fittings that will need attention – they should be removed, cleaned and rebedded on a marine-grade adhesive sealant, before being screwed or bolted back in position. The rubber or plastic seals on inspection hatches have only a finite life, so these may need to be replaced entirely.

If the problem is with the tanks,

Above: **Some inspection covers have a rubber seal that becomes perished over time. This is often sold as a spare.**

leaks are most likely to be where they join the hull or deck. These seams can be sealed by using the following method:

- ✿ Sand both sides of the join with a medium-grit abrasive paper.
- ✿ Thoroughly clean and dry the entire area.

Below: **Effective buoyancy is vital for all dinghies, to prevent the boat sinking in the event of a capsize or becoming swamped.**

TIP

The easiest way to add flotation to a boat that doesn't have enough, is to secure buoyancy bags underneath the thwarts. These can be fitted in minutes, are relatively cheap, and their condition is easy to check.

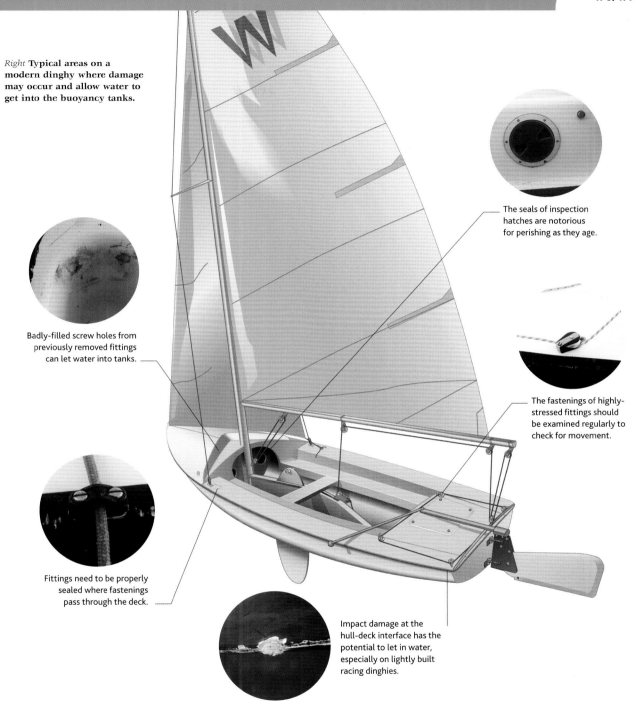

Right **Typical areas on a modern dinghy where damage may occur and allow water to get into the buoyancy tanks.**

The seals of inspection hatches are notorious for perishing as they age.

Badly-filled screw holes from previously removed fittings can let water into tanks.

The fastenings of highly-stressed fittings should be examined regularly to check for movement.

Fittings need to be properly sealed where fastenings pass through the deck.

Impact damage at the hull-deck interface has the potential to let in water, especially on lightly built racing dinghies.

● Laminate glassfibre tape over the top of the seam. Two layers are ample to create a strong join – use 25mm (1in) wide tape for the first layer and 50mm (2in) wide tape for the second. A neater job can be made if the glassfibre on each side is sanded away further, so that the repair lies below the height of the original gel coat.

● A new gel coat, which needs to be colour matched to the original, can then be applied and faired in so that it blends well with the original material.

Refastening loose fittings

Many dinghy deck fittings are subject to relatively small loads, and are therefore attached with self-tapping screws. However, if they pull out of the deck, some lateral thinking may be needed to refit them securely.

As a dinghy ages, the fastenings on the deck fittings inevitably experience movement when under load. This eventually leads to the screw holes becoming enlarged, and failing to grip. Simply replacing the screws with longer ones is often not feasible, as most fittings are designed for a certain size of fastening, so a larger one will not fit. In any case, this doesn't address the root cause of the problem.

If there's easy access behind the fitting, replacing screws with bolts and large washers is likely to be all that's needed. If there's no way of reaching the blind side of the fitting, an alternative that can work well for a wooden or heavily constructed glassfibre dinghy is to fill the old screw hole with a mix of resin and microfibres. As the resin starts to set, insert the screw to create a thread, then remove it before the epoxy hardens to prevent it becoming stuck in place.

This process may not, however, work with the thin laminates of modern lightweight racing dinghies. In some cases, the location will lend itself to cutting a hole for an inspection hatch, which will allow a hand to reach the blind side of the fitting. If this is not possible, though – either from a structural or aesthetic perspective – a marine plywood backing pad can be positioned behind the fitting, provided there's an inspection hatch within a couple of metres.

Start by running a mousing line from one of the screw holes to the hatch, as this can be used to pull the backing pad into place. Epoxy adhesive is squirted through the screw holes using a syringe, to fix the backing pad in place. The fitting can then be screwed to this, ensuring it's bedded down on a marine-grade sealant.

Below **Loose fittings should be attended to immediately. If left, screw holes will grow larger and a bigger repair will be needed.**

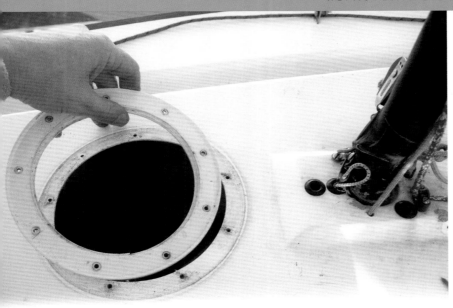

Aluminium spars

Screws or rivets that pull out of aluminium spars can also pose a problem, especially where corrosion of the metal is evident. It may be possible to bolt the fitting through the spar, but this risks further weakening, especially in highly stressed areas such as the gooseneck and the mid-section of a boom. A better solution is an aluminium backing plate, shaped to match the inside profile of the spar. This can be pre-drilled with holes for pop rivets, or bolts, and a thread tapped so there's no need for nuts on the blind side.

To fit the plate, take the end-cap off the spar, run a mousing line from the damaged screw holes, and pass the line through the fixing holes drilled in the backing plate. Then, use the mousing line to manoeuvre the plate into position, and fit the new bolts or rivets.

Above left **Leaking hatches are a common problem and can be solved by re-bedding with a marine-grade sealant.**

Above **These stainless steel self-tapping screws for a vang attachment have corroded the aluminium mast. As they are at the end of the spar, access is easy and they can be replaced with bolts.**

Resealing fittings

Mask around the edge of the fitting – this helps with cleaning up excess sealant.

Use a marine-grade adhesive sealant. This will last much longer than silicone types.

Apply a single bead that encircles the screw holes and links them together.

Rigging skills and repairing sails

The old adage that 'a stitch in time saves nine' is perhaps most fitting in relation to rigging and sail repairs. Regular inspections of the cloth and stitching will identify problems at an early stage, when only minimal remedial repairs are needed.

Sail repairs

In most cases with dinghy sails, self-adhesive patches are used to repair tears in the cloth or chafe – choose Dacron (polyester) or Mylar as appropriate for the construction of your sail. Lightweight spinnaker repair tape is sold in rolls of different colours to repair these sails.

The sail should first be washed with fresh water and then dried and de-greased using acetone. Rounding the corners of patches reduces localised stresses, helping them stay in place much longer.

If a large patch is needed in a high stress part of the sail – for instance, along the leech or near any corner reinforcement – then it may help to stitch the edge of the patch in place. Hand-stitching is viable for this, although a machine will make the job faster and neater. Many domestic machines will sew through two or three layers of Dacron sailcloth if fitted with a heavy denim needle.

Damaged stitching can easily be repaired by hand, simply by reusing the old needle holes. Double-sided tape is invaluable in holding the two panels in position so that the seam lies flat without puckering and doesn't move about as you stitch.

Repairing a torn sail

A pair of sailmaker's spikes is used to line up the two torn sections.

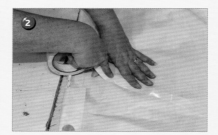

Double-sided adhesive tape is applied to both sides of the tear.

The edges of the patch are heat-sealed with an electric rope cutter.

Double-sided adhesive tape is applied to the edges of the patch.

The patch is stitched in place – either by machine or by hand.

The surplus thread is removed to leave a perfect finish.

Replacing a halyard

If a halyard has broken, and you need to replace it, you will have to drop a weighted messenger line down the mast via the upper halyard sheave. This can then be fished out of the lower sheave at the bottom of the mast, using stiff wire shaped into a hook. The new halyard can then be attached to the messenger line and pulled through the mast.

Alternatively, if the halyard to be replaced is still in one piece, attach the messenger line to the old halyard and pull it through the mast. The new halyard can then be attached to one end of the messenger line and pulled through.

Splicing an eye

Some ropes and control lines benefit from having a loop spliced in the end, rather than forming one with a knot. With modern braided rope this is straightforward, using a pointed hollow fid (needle). Start by separating the core of the rope from the sheath for about 30cm (12in) at the end of the rope, then follow the sequence shown below:

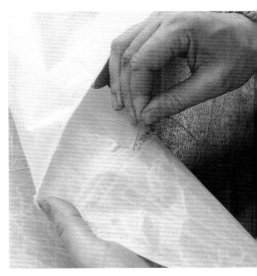

Right: **Each time you de-rig the boat, check the sails for any signs of damage.**

Braid on braid splice

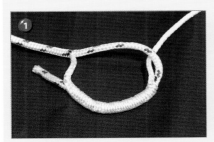

The (red & white) sheath has been pushed through the (white) core.

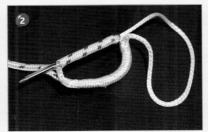

The fid (needle) provides a channel for the core to pass through part of the sheath.

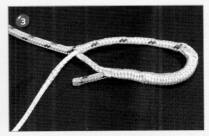

The core is pulled through the sheath until the slack is taken up.

The slack parts of the rope are now smoothed out.

The stainless steel thimble is fitted as the splice nears completion.

The surplus core is removed with an electric rope cutter.

Trailer care and repair

Boat trailers operate in a harsh environment and are often left languishing without care for long periods. If they are left standing for a long time, they should be inspected thoroughly, and any problems fixed.

To prolong the life of the wheel bearings as well as the structure of the trailer itself it should ideally never be immersed in water – that's the function of the separate launching trolley. Most boat trailers are made from mild steel that's prevented from rusting by good paintwork or by galvanising. The latter has a longer lifespan, but in both cases rust will eventually eat into the trailer, eventually affecting its structural integrity.

Tapping the trailer's framework with a small hammer will give you an indication of its condition – if the metal is sound, it will ring like a bell, with a clear note. However, if only a dull thud is heard, a considerable amount of corrosion may be present.

Couplings

A hitch that hooks on to your vehicle's towbar should be easy to use and freshly greased. If it has seized, either partially or fully, it's worth soaking the moving parts in penetrating oil or diesel to see whether they can be coaxed into movement.

Breakaway cables and security couplings are simple safety devices that are crucial in the event of a trailer becoming separated from its towing vehicle, yet are often missing or defective. A security coupling is used on unbraked trailers – this is a length of wire with a loop at each end, one attached to the trailer and the other hooked over the towing vehicle's towbar. If the trailer's coupling unhitches itself, the trailer will still be attached to the towing vehicle via the security wire. Braked trailers are fitted with a breakaway cable that applies the trailer's brakes should the trailer become detached from the tow vehicle.

Above: **Lighting boards are subject to a lot of vibration, especially on empty trailers, so bulb failure is common.**

TIP

Many boat trailers cover very small mileages, so tyres are more likely to succumb to the ravages of time than the tread wearing out. Any tyre that's more than ten years old should therefore be replaced.

Below: **Don't be complacent about the condition of your trailer – it needs to be checked regularly.**

Suspension units are normally sealed items that require no routine servicing. But, they are made from painted or galvanised steel, so it's vital to check periodically that these are rust-free and in good condition, and touch up any damaged paint.

Braking systems

Most dinghy trailers do not need an integral breaking system, except in the rare cases where the boat weighs more than around 400kg (900lb), or if the trailer is designed to transport multiple dinghies. Many boat trailers rely on braking systems designed for trailers that are never submersed in water. This means cables are prone to corrosion, and can jam in their outer sleeves. Components may also seize within the brake drum. The only remedy for this is to replace the cable, or strip the brake system apart.

Storing trailers

If a trailer is to be stored for any length of time, start by giving it a full service to minimise the deterioration of key parts such as brakes and wheel bearings. Lift the trailer on a jack, and place chocks beneath it to take the strain off the tyres and suspension units. Where fitted, the brake should also be released.

When recommissioning a trailer it's vital to ensure it's in a fully roadworthy condition. If it was decommissioned as above, a check of the wheel bearings, braking system and condition of the chassis and suspension units is likely to be all that's required. However, if the trailer's history is unknown, a full service, covering the structure, wheel bearings, suspension units, brakes (where fitted), tyres, lights, tow hitch and security coupling or breakaway cable, should be done.

Above: **Examining the condition of the security coupling of a small, non-braked trailer. This stops it breaking free if the tow hitch fails.**

Right: **Never assume a trailer, however new, is roadworthy. The suspension units of this two-year-old trailer already have significant corrosion visible.**

Glossary

A

abeam At a right-angle to the length of the boat.

aft Towards the rear (or stern) of the boat.

ahead Forwards movement, or in front of the boat.

anchor A heavy metal object designed to help to hold a boat in its position.

apparent wind The direction of the wind as it appears when the boat is moving.

astern Backwards movement, or behind the boat.

B

backing An anti-clockwise shift in the wind direction. The opposite of 'veering'.

backwinded When the wind pushes on the wrong side of the sail, either directly or reflected off another sail.

bail To remove water from a boat, normally using a pump, scoop or bucket.

balance When the boat is in perfect balance and there is no pull on the tiller.

battens Battens are attached to a sail to stiffen the leech to make a better sail shape.

beam The width of a boat.

beam reach A point of sail where the apparent wind is coming from the beam (side) of the yacht.

bear away Alter course by swinging the boat's bow away from the wind.

bearing The direction, usually measured in degrees, of a fixed point or another vessel.

beating Pointing as close to the wind as the boat will sail.

Beaufort scale A method of measuring the force of wind, named after Admiral Beaufort who created the system.

block One or more wheels free to spin between parallel 'cheeks'. Used to change the direction of a rope's travel and often to increase mechanical advantage.

boom The spar to which the foot, or bottom, of the mainsail is attached.

boom vang (or vang) A method used to hold down the boom, to help it maintain a good sail shape. See also 'kicking strap' and 'gnav'.

bow The front, or forward end, of the boat.

bowline A knot used to make a loop at the end of a line.

broad reach Sailing with the apparent wind coming across the aft quarter of the boat.

bungs Closure for small opening that allows buoyancy tanks (or the cockpit) to be drained after sailing. Bungs must be inserted before launching.

buoy A floating device used as a navigational aid.

C

cam cleat A cleat (fitting) used to hold a line. It uses two spring-loaded cams that come together to clamp firmly on the line.

capsize When a boat turns over in the water and lies on its side.

catamaran A twin-hulled boat.

centreboard A retractable keel that slots into the hull of a dinghy, and hinges backwards.

channel A safe route on a waterway, usually marked by buoys.

channel marker A buoy or other mark used to indicate the edge of a channel.

chart datum The water level used to record data on a chart. It is defined as the depth of water at the lowest astronomical tide.

chine The joint between two flat panels on the hull - typically where the bottom of a plywood dinghy meets the topsides of the hull.

cleat A fitting to which lines can be easily attached.

clew Lower aft corner of a sail.

close-hauled To sail as close to the direction of the wind as possible.

close-reach Sailing with the wind coming from forward of the beam.

close-winded A boat that is able to sail close to the direction from which the wind is blowing.

clove hitch A knot formed either at the end or in the middle of a rope, best when strain will be equal on both sides.

cold front A mass of cold air moving towards a mass of warm air. Normally associated with strong winds and rain.

come about To tack. To change a boat's direction, bringing the bow through the wind.

compass rose A circle on a chart indicating the direction of true and magnetic north.

course The direction the boat is going in.

cringle A large eyelet, typically in a sail, through which a line can be passed.

cunningham A line used to control the tension along a sail's luff in order to maintain proper sail shape.

D

Dacron A synthetic polyester material often used for sail cloth.

daggerboard Similar to a centreboard, but raised vertically. It prevents a dinghy being pushed sideways by the wind.

distress signal Any signal used to indicate that a vessel is in distress.

downhaul A line used to pull down on a spar or sail.

downwind In the direction the wind is blowing.

E

eye-splice A loop formed at the end of a rope by turning the end back and splicing it to the main part of the rope.

F

fairlead A ring that diverts the route of a rope to ensure it is free of obstructions.

figure-of-eight A knot used at the end of a sheet as a stopper.

foil A rudder, centreboard or daggerboard.

foot The bottom edge of a sail.

footstrap A strap attached to the cockpit to put feet under when hiking, if sailing a dinghy.

foredeck The front of a boat, ahead of the mast.

forward Towards, or near, the front of the boat.

furl To roll a sail in.

G

gel coat A protective layer of resin on a GRP hull.

Global Positioning System (GPS) A system of satellites that allows a boat's position to be calculated with great accuracy using an electronic receiver.

gnav An 'inverse' kicking strap or vang fitted above the boom that presses the boom downwards. Has the advantage that it leaves more clear space in the cockpit. See also 'boom vang' and 'kicking strap'.

go about To tack.

gooseneck Hinged fitting which attaches the boom to the mast.

goosewinging Sailing with the wind behind and the jib held out to the opposite side of the mainsail.

gybe To turn the boat so that the stern swings across the direction of the wind.

H

half hitch A simple knot usually used with another knot or with a half hitch.

halyard Rope used to pull sails up the mast.

hank Sprung metal fitting that attaches a non-furling sail to a stay.

head Top corner of a sail.

headboard Reinforcing at the head of a sail.

heading The direction you are sailing at any given time.

head-to-wind When the bow of the boat is in the direction that the wind is coming from.

head up To turn the bow more directly into the wind.

heeling When a boat leans sideways, caused by pressure of wind against the sails.

helm The tiller of a dinghy.

helmsman The person who is on the helm and steering the boat.

high tide The point when the tide is at its highest.

hiking Sitting out over the side to counteract the heeling of a boat.

hitch A knot used to attach a line to any fixture, or back to itself.

hoist To raise a sail.

hull The main structural body of the boat.

I

isobars Lines drawn on a weather map (synoptic chart) indicating regions of equal pressure.

J

jib A small triangular sail at the front of the boat.

jib sheets Ropes used to control the jib after hoisting the sail.

K

kicking strap A control line from the mast to the underside of the boom, used to hold the boom down. See also 'boom vang'.

knot The nautical measurement of speed. A speed of one knot is one nautical mile per hour.

L

launch To put a boat in the water.

lee shore The shore that the wind is blowing towards.

leech The rear edge of a sail.

leech line A line used to tighten the leech of a sail, helping to create good sail shape.

leeward The direction away from the wind. Opposite of windward.

leeway The sideways movement of a boat away from the wind.

lifejacket A device used to keep a person afloat. Also called a PFD (personal flotation device).

low tide The point when the tide is at its lowest.

luff Front edge of a sail.

luffing Term used when the front of a sail has lost power and is flapping.

M

magnetic course A yacht's course measured in degrees from the earth's magnetic pole.

magnetic north The direction to which a magnetic compass points.

magnetic variation The difference between magnetic north and true north, measured as an angle.

mainsail The principal sail set on the main mast.

mainsheet The line used to control the mainsail.

MAYDAY An internationally recognised distress signal used on a radio to indicate a life-threatening situation.

minute One minute is 1/60 of one degree; a minute of latitude is the equivalent of one nautical mile.

monohull A boat with one hull.

multihull Any boat with more than one hull, such as a catamaran or trimaran.

N

nautical mile Measurement of distance at sea. A nautical mile is equivalent to about 1.15 statute miles (6067.12ft) or 1,852 metres. A minute of latitude is equal to one nautical mile.

neap tide The tide with the least variation in water level. The lowest high tide and the highest low tide occur at neap tide.

O

offshore wind Wind that is blowing away from the land, towards the water; opposite of 'onshore'

outboard engine An engine used to power a small boat. Outboard engines are normally mounted on a bracket on the stern.

outhaul A line used to tension the foot of a sail.

P

painter A line attached to the bow of a dinghy and used to tie it up or tow it.

pinching Steering too close to the wind, causing the sails to luff.

pintle A pin used to attach a stern-mounted rudder.

planing A boat rising slightly out of the water so that it is gliding over the water at speed, rather than through it.

plot To find a boat's actual or intended course or mark a position on a chart.

point of sail The angle of a yacht or dinghy in relation to the wind.

port The left side of the boat from the perspective of a person standing at the stern of the boat and looking towards the bow.

port tack Sailing with the wind coming over the port side and the boom on the starboard side of the boat.

R

reaching Any point of sail with the wind coming from the side of the boat.

reef To partially lower and furl a sail so that its area is smaller.

reefing lines Lines used to pull the reef into the sail.

rigging Both the permanent wires which support a boat's mast(s) and to which the sails are attached (standing rigging), and the wires and/or ropes used to hoist and control the sails (running rigging).

roach A curve out from the aft edge (leech) of a sail. Battens help support and stiffen the roach.

rudder A flat structure attached behind or underneath the stern used to control the direction in which the boat is travelling.

running A point of sail where the boat has the wind coming from behind the vessel.

S

sail trim The position of the sails relative to the wind and desired point of sail.

satellite navigation Navigation using information transmitted from satellites.

shackle A metal, U-shaped connector that is attached to other fittings by a pin inserted through the arms of the 'U'.

sheets Ropes used to control a sail once it is hoisted.

shroud Part of the standing rigging that helps to support the mast by running from the top of the mast to the side of the boat.

skiff A modern, lightweight, powerful and very fast dinghy.

sounding The depth of the water as marked on a chart.

spar Any metal or wooden pole used to help set a sail.

spinnaker A large, lightweight sail used at the bow when running or on reaching.

spinnaker pole A pole used to extend the foot of the spinnaker beyond the edge of the boat, and to secure the corner of the sail.

spreaders Small spars extending towards the sides of the boat from one or more places along the mast. The shrouds attach to the end of the spreaders, so that the shrouds can support the mast.

spring tide The tide with the most variation in water level, eg the highest high tide and the lowest low tide.

squall A sudden intense wind storm, usually with rain showers; often associated with a cold front.

starboard The right side of a boat, from the stern of the boat looking forwards.

starboard tack Sailing so that the wind is coming over the starboard side and the boom is on the port side.

stern The back, or aft end, of a boat.

T

tack (1) The direction a boat is sailing with respect to the wind. (2) To change a boat's direction by bringing the bow through the wind. (3) Bottom front corner of a sail.

telltale A short length of light line, cloth or wool attached near the luff of a sail, to indicate air flow and thus aid the correct sail trim.

thwart A seat running across the width of a small boat.

tidal atlas Small charts showing directions and rates of tidal flow, over a period of hours.

tidal range The difference between a tide's high and low water levels.

tidal stream The movement of water caused by the rise and fall of tidal waters.

tide The regular rising and lowering of water in parts of the world due to the pull of the sun and the moon.

tidetables Tables containing information about the time of the high and low tides and the water level to be expected at that time.

tiller An arm attached to the top of the rudder to steer a boat.

tiller extension An extension to the tiller allowing the helmsman to steer while hiking. Also known as a hiking stick.

transit Two navigation aids or other fixed points which can be lined up one behind the other. When they are in line, the boat must be somewhere along this line.

transom The aft end of the hull.

trapeze Wire supporting the weight of crew or helmsman, enabling them to put their entire body weight outside the boat to balance the vessel.

trim To haul in on a sheet to adjust the sail angle.

trimaran A boat with a central hull and two smaller outer hulls.

true course The course of a boat after being corrected for magnetic deviation and magnetic variation.

true wind The speed and direction of the wind, in relation to a static object.

U

upwind To windward, in the direction from which the wind is blowing.

V

vang See 'boom vang', 'gnav' and 'kicking strap'.

veering A clockwise shift in wind direction; opposite of 'backing'.

VHF Very High Frequency radio waves. VHF radios are the most common ones carried on boats.

W

weather helm The tendency of a boat to head up towards the wind.

windward The direction from which the wind is blowing.

Index

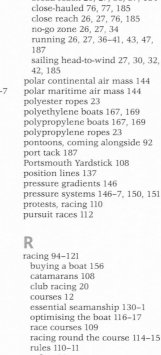